MATER

MEXICO

LAND OF
MARY'S
WONDERS

MEXICO
LAND OF

St. Anthony Guild Press, Paterson, New Jersey

MARY'S
WONDERS

Joseph L. Cassidy

Priest of the Archdiocese of Newark

Nihil obstat:

BEDE BABO, O. S. B.

Censor

Imprimatur:

✝ JAMES A. MCNULTY

Bishop of Paterson

June 30, 1958

PRINTED IN THE UNITED STATES OF AMERICA

Dedicated

in admiration and reverence

to those missioners who brought the Faith to Mexico

and fostered devotion to the Blessed Virgin

in the

Land of

Mary's Wonders

FOREWORD

Tertullian tells us that God is concerned, in all His Being, to show forth His attributes in all their perfection, lovingly tracing their outlines and delineating their form. (*Liber de Resurrectione,* Can. 6, 9). Thus, when God created man, He endowed him carefully and lovingly with certain perfections, because man is a creature, as the Scriptures tell us, in His own "image and likeness."

When an artist paints or fashions an image, he does it carefully, so that the work may truly represent the idea in his mind and at the same time manifest to the world his own ability as painter or sculptor. Thus, it seems likely in the case of painted or sculptured images of Jesus Christ, the Son of God, that God is concerned to secure for these images the veneration due them as likenesses of Himself. He desires them to conform to the Divine Original. But each artist is free to delineate the Divine perfections according to his own personal conception of them. Therefore this conformity which God seeks between Himself and man-made images of Him must be not primarily in their physical likeness, but in their powers to do good. As Saint John Chrysostom says, speaking of God and His image: *"Ego vero utroque nomine Deum admiror"* — "Under either name it is God I envisage."

The Blessed Virgin Mary, as the most perfect of God's creatures, is the most perfect created likeness, or image, of the Divine perfections, and consequently, after God Himself, must be deserving of the highest veneration, or hyperdulia. Carrying the parallel one step further, to the paintings and sculptures of the Virgin Mary there should be accorded a reverence second only to that due to the images of her Divine Son.

Now if God is concerned to show forth His attributes in Mary, the most perfect of His creatures, we may say that it is

most fitting for those images of her to be endowed with mani-
festations of her most perfect creature attributes. And we may
piously believe that, through those images of Mary which are
venerated as miraculous, or wonderworking, the Blessed Virgin
deigns to help us.

One to whom a religious art-form fails to communicate
its fundamental message may tend to undervalue the religious sentiment that inspired it. Those of us who are accustomed to seeing images of the Child Jesus dressed in a long
singlet may find *El Santo Niño de Atocha* incapable of inspir-
ing devotion. Yet to the Indian, there is nothing strange about
vesting *El Niño* in the gold brocade, plumed hat, and buckled
shoes of a sixteenth-century Spanish nobleman — nor even, as
I have seen Him, as a Mexican *charro,* with silver-embroidered
suit and broad-brimmed hat, fancy *charro* boots and *riata!*
And to a copper-hued race, who affectionately call the Virgin
of Tepeyac *La Morenita* ("The Little Dark One"), it is the
most natural thing in the world that Our Lady of Guadalupe
should have the type of beauty that they look for in their own
daughters.

Confronted with the reaction of some who mistake the
canons of art for the criteria of devotion, we should do well
to keep in mind the words of Saint John of the Cross: "If
God sometimes shows mercies and works miracles, *ordinarily*
He does it through the medium of images neither very well
carved nor curiously painted or appareled. . . . And many times
Our Lord grants these favors by means of those images which
are in out-of-the-way or lonely places. The very fact of going
to visit them serves to increase the affection and intensifies the
act of piety." Viewed in this light, the pilgrimages to the
sacred shrines of Christendom take on a deeper meaning.

Before we describe the many wonderful occurrences attributed to Mary through her various representations at the shrines

of Mexico, it may be well to consider the proper attitude in the presence of miraculous events, in order to avoid a double pitfall: skepticism, and credulity.

No supernatural wonders are ever wrought without an important spiritual reason: they are intended as signs to lead men to a greater love of God. That these signs take the form of externally sensible marvels is due to the fact that man, in his present condition, is living in a material world, where the only signs accessible to him, outside of a very rare direct communication of God to the soul, are to be found in such physical happenings.

Miracles always have two elements: one external, visible, and perceptible to all, and one internal, which consists in graces and intimate dispositions of the soul. Any retelling of such miracles has to bear mostly upon the external happenings, since spiritual graces are generally personal and hidden. In some cases, however, they become apparent; for example, the mass conversion of Indians in Mexico after the apparitions and miracles of Guadalupe.

If the hidden spiritual effects are not constantly kept in mind, a succession of such wondrous events as healings, rainfalls, or miraculous preservations of images may appear to be so materialistic as to be quite unrelated to religion, and to be nothing but the product of the imagination of a childlike people. On the other hand, a too intense devotion to a statue as an exclusive provider of health, wealth, and happiness may easily lead to superstitious credulity.

It is most important to remember that between these two extremes there is much to be found in the favors poured upon the shrines of Mary in Mexico: the tenderness and love of God and of His Blessed Mother. To be sure, many of the occurrences appear as somewhat simple and materialistic. Before the missionaries brought Christianity to Mexico, the pagan priests also prayed for rain and healing. But we should remember that the principal beneficiaries of these wonders are the descendants of these same Indians, spiritually simple children led to God precisely through the fulfillment of some of their material needs. An important first task of the missionary is to feed, clothe, and heal; not strange, then, that Mary's predilection for the people of Mexico should at times manifest itself in the bestowal of material favors. If, as is evident, these sensible, material favors should lead people to grow in grace and virtue, there is nothing about them to cause disbelief.

The true Catholic attitude toward the veneration of images was clearly defined at the end of the period of Iconoclasm by the Second Council of Nicæa, in the year 787: "Images of Christ, and of His Virgin Mother and of other saints are to be made and to be kept, and due honor and veneration is to be given them; not that any divinity or virtue is believed to be in them on account of which they would have to be honored, or that any prayer is to be addressed to them, or that any confidence is to be placed in them, as was formerly done by the heathens, who placed their hopes in idols: but because the honor which is given them is referred to the originals which they represent; so that by kissing the images, by uncovering our heads or kneeling before them, we adore Christ and venerate His saints, whose likeness they represent" (Session 25).

No occurrence described in this book is a matter of absolute faith, even those officially recognized by the Church. As indicated in each individual case, either they are based on solid historical testimony and thus should be accorded the same degree of credence and respect as historically verifiable data in any other field; or they are to be prudently regarded only as pious legends with no more authority than other such traditions.

It is not the aim of this book, nor within the competency of the writer, to prove that one or other of the events narrated, whether qualified as fact, tradition, or legend, is a true miracle; such matters are the province of the ecclesiastical authorities.

Apropos of this question, however, the words of the learned Father Feijoó are of interest. Writing in Spain during the eighteenth century, in his *Cartas Eruditas y Curiosas* Father Feijoó says:

"Naturally, you wish some rule to distinguish supernatural cures from those due to nature or to medicine. I cannot give you one more adequate or more sure than that published by our Holy Father Benedict XIV while still Cardinal, shortly before ascending the Papal throne, in the fourth book of his great work *De Servorum Dei Beatificatione et Beatorum Canonizatione . . . ,* consisting of these conditions: 1) That the illness cured be grave and naturally incurable, or at least curable only with difficulty; 2) That it be not lessening; 3) That no remedies shall have been tried, or if tried, shall have been ineffective; 4) That the cure be sudden or instantaneous, and at the same time complete and perfect; 5) That it shall not have been preceded by a natural crisis; 6) That it be constant, or lasting — that is, without any relapse." Father Feijoó then adds: "When you find a cure which fulfills the above conditions, and furnish me with sufficient testimony thereto, I shall be the first to declare that it is miraculous. And if I find a thousand which meet the above requirements, of every one of the thousand I shall declare the same" (*Carta XLIII,* par. 10 and 11).

When we dwell on the prodigious or marvelous elements in the history of Mary's images, it is not to cater to men's appetite for the unusual, but to inspire a closer acquaintance with Our Lady herself. When we recount the history of her shrines, it is to induce a more profound understanding, in so far as may be allowed us here, of Mary's perfections. Saint Augustine tells us that miracles speak to us in their own language and we must ask them what they are saying. What lesson does Mary want to teach us in each miracle that has occurred in connection with her shrines and images?

Having made these necessary distinctions, the important fact remains that Mexico is a land with deep and widespread devotion to Mary, a land much beloved by her, where woman is respected and the mother holds her humble yet triumphant place in the home — truly a LAND OF MARY'S WONDERS.

— THE AUTHOR

Feast of Our Lady of Lourdes, 1958
Santa Úrsula Xitla
Tlalpan, D. F., Mexico

CONTENTS

OUR LADY OF THE IMMACULATE CONCEPTION

Aguascalientes, Aguascalientes

I

LA PURISIMA DE SAN DIEGO

(OUR LADY OF THE IMMACULATE CONCEPTION)

Aguascalientes, Aguascalientes

SOME 365 miles north of Mexico City, on the road to El Paso, is Aguascalientes, the capital of the State of Aguascalientes. This city has long been celebrated for its climate, which is practically the same all year round, and for the thermal baths ("hot waters") for which it was named. Pedro de Alvarado, that intrepid lieutenant of Hernán Cortés, explored the region as early as 1522, and according to legend left a fortune in treasure buried in a nearby mountain. So far as is known, the first European actually to set foot on the site of the present city was Don Pedro Alméndez Chirinos, who, under orders from Nuño de Guzman, led an expedition through that area in 1531, and in his report mentioned the hot water springs. In 1575 a decree of Philip II authorized the founding of a town there, to be dedicated to Mary under the title *La Asunción de Aguascalientes* ("Our Lady of the Assumption of Aguascalientes"). In 1611 the Crown raised it to the status of town of the first class, with the title, *La Villa de Nuestra Señora de la Asunción de Aguascalientes.* Finally, in 1824, it achieved the rank of *ciudad* — city.

From its earliest Spanish beginnings, then, Aguascalientes has been dedicated to the Assumption of Our Lady. So it is

1

not strange to find that devotion to her is widespread, not only in the capital, but in the entire state. This devotion centers primarily about an image of the Immaculate Conception, venerated in the old Franciscan Church of San Diego, and known affectionately as *La Purísima* ("Mary Most Pure"). It is eminently true, as Fray Angel Ochoa, O. F. M., has asserted, that "devotion to the Immaculate Conception in Aguascalientes is directly connected with the work of the Franciscans there." Of the five names which history relates in the founding of the *Villa* of Aguascalientes in 1611, one was a Franciscan, Fray Gabriel de Jesus.

Aguascalientes is indebted to a Don Pedro Rincón de Ortega for the còming of the Franciscans to the city. An early church and convent in the custody of the Discalced Carmelites having been left vacant, Don Pedro petitioned the Bishop of Guadalajara, Don Juan Ruiz Colmenero, who wrote to Philip IV of Spain about the matter in 1653. His Majesty granted the request, and the Franciscans of San Diego were entrusted with the church and convent, finally taking possession on the twenty-fifth of January, 1664, with Don Pedro Rincón de Ortega, who had the *patronado* of the convent, making the presentation to the Franciscan *Definidores,* Fray Cristóbal Muñoz de la Concepción and Fray Martín de Vadiola. The contemporary document recording the ceremony throws an interesting light on the manner in which such business was transacted:

" . . . Standing at the door of the Convent of Our Lady of the Conception on the outskirts of this Villa, in the presence of *Licenciado* Don Pedro Rincón de Ortega, patron of the said convent, Fray Xobl. Muños de la Concepción, *Predicador* and *Definidor* of the holy province of San Diego, handed over to me the acts and writs, with the manuscript of foundation contained in this petition; and in virtue of the same he requested me to give him possession of the subrogation in the said convent. And to the Father *Presidente,* the aforenamed Fray Martín de Vadiola, who was present, I made over the buildings and the servants. Accordingly the said Fathers, in token of possession, locked and unlocked the doors of the said church, and entered it, accompanied by a great gathering of people, chanting the *Te Deum Laudamus....*"

Earliest Franciscan documents show that the image of *La Purísima* — the Immaculate Conception — was in the church as early as 1665, for in that year Don Pedro Rincón contributed an alms of fifty pesos toward its cost, and the entire cost of the image is given as one hundred thirty pesos. Another record of the convent, listing the appurtenances of the church, describes the statue as "an image of the Immaculate Conception of Our Lady, two *varas* in height" — about sixty-seven inches.

As years went by, Aguascalientes grew apace. Other religious orders came to minister to the increasing population. Many new churches came to be constructed, and within the framework of the Faith, other devotions grew in popularity and intensity. But through all the progress and change which marked the city's growth, the *cultus* of the Immaculate Conception remained the principal devotion of the citizens. The Third Order of Saint Francis, established there in 1664, frequently carried the venerable image through the city in public procession, a testimonial in which the rest of the city readily joined. In 1723 an annual procession through the streets of the city was decreed, to be held on the eighth of December, Feast of the Immaculate Conception, and the members of the Third Order were directed to carry lighted candles.

With the passage of time, and as a result of the constant exposure to the elements, the original statue of the Immaculate Conception deteriorated. Finally, something under a century after the Franciscan foundation of San Diego, the image was replaced by another, the one which today is venerated in the same temple.

Speak to the citizens of Aguascalientes and you will hear enthusiastic tales about the advent of the image of Our Lady to their city. For a fee, tourist guides will regale you with marvelous legends relating to the image — few of them worthy of credence, it must be said. One legend affirms that a mule laden with a heavy box came to the doors of the church and fell upon its knees. When the box was opened, the head and hands of the present statue were discovered. Another legend tells of a missionary friar who came to the Convent of San Diego one night for shelter and rest in the course of his journeyings. He carried with him a case which contained the head and hands for an image he proposed to set up at the site of his mission. The following morning, when he did not appear for the community Mass, a friar went to wake him, and found the missionary kneeling before the box, having died at prayer during the night.

A more likely version can be substantiated by historical data. The necrology of San Diego refers to Fray Lorenzo de Rueda, who died there on the twenty-eighth of October, 1781. According to tradition, it was he who brought the image to San Diego, after a shipwreck had frustrated his design of sending it to one of the convents of the Order in Europe. As Fray Lorenzo de Rueda was Guardian of the Convent of San Diego in 1775, exactly one hundred years after the founding, it appears probable that the newer image was already in Aguascalientes by that time. Nevertheless, the image apparently was not placed in the church for public veneration until after Fray Lorenzo's death in 1781.

In the history of devotion to the Blessed Virgin in Mexico there are many instances on record of popular refusal to accept a new image in place of an older one. Such, however, does not seem to have been the case in regard to the image of *La Purísima de San Diego*. A partial explanation of this fact may lie in the remarkable beauty of the statue. We do not have any extant likenesses of the earlier image, though from available data it was of local origin. The present image, on the other hand, is undoubtedly of the school of Guatemala, noted for the beauty and mysticism of expression which its artists were able to infuse into their work. Not surprisingly, then, the devotion and love of the faithful increased with the coming of the new *Purísima*. A greater enthusiasm than ever manifested itself in the annual processions, as well as in the eight days of prayer which annually precede the Feast of the Immaculate Conception.

When the struggle for independence rocked Mexico, the people of Aguascalientes, like those in other cities of the country, had to pay dearly for their loyalty to the Faith. Religion was attacked on all sides, and with the advent of the Reform period, and the Constitution, as the political leaders strove to advance the political rights of man, they seemed to trample underfoot his right and duty to worship God. It is understandable, then, that in the midst of this era of spiritual confusion, a series of catastrophes should have served to call men back to a sense of their dependence upon a Power higher than the state.

From these events, Aguascalientes was not exempt. In 1833 an epidemic of cholera swept through the city beginning in the middle of May, and by the end of August the daily death toll had reached two hundred. In this calamity, hearts once more turned heavenward, imploring the Divine Mercy. With a sense of their common misfortune, people approached *La Purísima* with renewed devotion, beseeching Our Lady to turn away the scourge. The venerable image was carried in public procession through the city, and a solemn triduum — three days of prayer and penance — was celebrated in the parish church. Against all the pronouncements of the medical profession, which saw in these public gatherings only an occasion for further spreading of the plague, a notable decrease in mortality ensued. A solemn procession of thanksgiving conducted *La Purísima* back to her own sanctuary in San Diego.

In the cholera epidemic of 1850, the intercession of *La Purísima* was besought once more. This time the city was stricken for ten months, and according to a contemporary historian, the population of Aguascalientes was reduced 80 per cent. As in the great plague of Egypt, hardly a family in the city but was in mourning, and the remedies of medical science were apparently ineffectual. Again the image of *La Purísima* was taken in procession through the city, and a solemn novena held in the principal church. Tradition relates that at once a notable decrease in sickness and mortality was experienced.

When the plagues had been conquered, the people of Aguascalientes did not forget their debt to *La Purísima,* but in grateful memory continued the processions year after year. The diary of an old priest, writing of a procession on the twenty-sixth of July, 1855, bears striking witness to the enthusiasm and devotion which flourished around *La Purísima* at that time:

" . . . I feared last night, upon entering (the church) that the image of Our Lady would fall to the ground, the way the press of people was knocking me about. More than once I sought to devise a means of restraining the crowd, which kept pushing and shoving while we three chaplains went to receive the sacred image. Only a guard of armed troops could keep order, but I am not disposed to have recourse to this means for the present."

Although the enthusiastic votaries did not know it, they were witnessing the last public procession of their beloved *Purísima* through the streets of Aguascalientes. The Constitution of 1857 was to outlaw such public acts of worship. In 1857, too, the Franciscan Province of San Diego was dissolved, and the church came to form part of the present-day Province of San Francisco and San Diego of Jalisco. Never again was the Province of San Diego to resume its independence, though a number of the *Dieguiños* continued to serve, under the new administration, at the convent and temple of their original foundation.

During the *Carrancista* revolt, when the churches were closed and pillaged of their treasures, *La Purísima* went into hiding. The *Presidente* of the convent, Fray Bernardino Madueño, substituted another image. Whether the substitute was the ancient, original sculpture or another similar to it is not known. As the Church of San Diego did not open for public worship throughout this period, the faithful as a whole were unaware of the change. When, however, the church was finally reopened for religious services, the venerable *Purísima* returned to her shrine.

In 1924, a curious incident highlighted the special veneration which *La Purísima* enjoys among the people. In the course of time the image had deteriorated to some extent, and the authorities of San Diego decided to have it entirely retouched. To this end a substitute statue was placed in the niche, and *La Purísima* was taken to the sacristy and placed in charge of a sculptor. The triduum preceding the fifteenth of August — Feast of the Assumption of Our Lady — arrived. The people, seeing the niche covered and a strange image of the Virgin on view, assumed that *La Purísima* had been removed to be garbed in festal robes. But when the Feast of the Assumption came and within the niche appeared a statue other than their be-

loved *Purísima,* the faithful began to make inquiries. When
they found that the image of *La Purísima* had been removed
for retouching, they were furious. Crowds stormed the doors
of the convent demanding to see the image, to assure themselves that it had not been harmed. Those who were able to
make their way into the sacristy gathered fragments or splin-
ters of wood which had been cut from the body of the image
in the course of the retouching, and treasured them as precious
relics. Not satisfied with the explanation offered by the Su-
perior of the convent, they went to the civil authorities. Fear-
ful for the peace and order of the city, the governor of the
state, through his attorney general, telegraphed to the Provincial of the Franciscans, requesting him to return the image to
its shrine in the interest of public order. The wish of the civil
authorities was complied with, and the work stopped before
the features of the venerable statue had been retouched. From
that time on, no attempt has been made to change *La Purísima*
in any way. The faithful of Aguascalientes, like loving children, prefer to see the image of their Heavenly Mother growing old gracefully, without having recourse to modern cosmetic
processes of artificial beautification.

Thus the image of *La Purísima* of San Diego may be seen
today substantially as it came from the hands of the sculptor
almost two hundred years ago. Standing slightly over sixty-
eight inches in height, from the crown of the head to the feet,
it is a perfectly proportioned sculpture. From elbow to elbow
it measures about nineteen inches, and the face, from hairline
to chin, just over nine and one-half inches. The face is inclined gently to the left, and the eyes, deep brown in color,
look down into the face of one who prays before the shrine.
The beautifully formed hands are lightly joined at the palms
and fingertips. The feet are sandaled, the left one somewhat
advanced and with heel slightly raised. The image stands upon

a half-globe supported by two seraphim; the globe is now usually hidden by the flowing vestments of the image. Before the feet is a crescent, star-tipped moon. Upon the head is a golden, jewel-encrusted crown.

The *camarín* of *La Purísima* contains many sets of vestments, which are changed according to the feast or season. *La Purísima's* jewel case, filled by the devotion of two centuries, contains many precious jewels, necklaces of pearl, rings and earrings, all of which are used at various times.

As we have said, experts classify the image of *La Purísima* as a product of the school of Guatemala, which developed the finest sculptors and sculptures in the New World. The sculptors of this school employed special coloring materials, as well as a distinctive technique for polishing the face and hands of the figure. One of the secrets of the remarkable finish they obtained was the lacquer, prepared with ceruse of Venetian silver, in a formula which, since their time, has never been successfully duplicated.

Even more important, from the standpoint of the devotee, is the expression which the school of Guatemala succeeded in imparting to the features, an expression at once warm and filled with mysticism, which is a characteristic of the *Guatemalteco* sculptors. Some slight marks, as of abrasion, are observable upon the face, possibly incurred during the period when the statue was hidden away; otherwise the features are perfectly preserved.

On the eighth of November, 1954, during the centenary observance of the dogmatic definition of the Immaculate Conception, *La Purísima* of San Diego was solemnly crowned with the golden crown she now wears. This occasion marked the rise of an even greater devotion to the Virgin Mary in Aguascalientes. There can be no doubt that, in the hearts of its citizens, *La Purísima* truly enjoys the title by which she has

long been venerated in the ancient and still-popular novena to
the Immaculate Conception used today in that city: *Reina y
Madre de Aguascalientes* — that is, "Queen and Mother of
Aguascalientes."

OUR LADY OF GUADALUPE
Villa de Guadalupe, D. F.

II

NUESTRA SEÑORA DE GUADALUPE

(OUR LADY OF GUADALUPE)

Villa de Guadalupe, D. F.

*M*EXICO. The year of Our Lord 1531. Ten years and four months before, Hernán Cortés had accomplished the subjugation of the proud Aztec nation. And now, scarcely a decade later, a million and a half of the indigenous population had already embraced baptism and the Faith of Christ. On the ninth day of December in the year we speak of, one of these Indians, Juan Diego by name, left his humble dwelling in Cuautitlán. Juan was on his way to hear Mass at the Church of Santiago, in the barrio of Tlaltelolco. His way led past a hill called by the Indians Tepeyacac, and as dawn was breaking he arrived at the foot of the hill.

Suddenly there came to his ears the sound of sweet singing, like the voices of birds myriad and various, singing together with such ineffable harmony that the Indian was overcome with wonder and delight. Raising his eyes to the summit of Tepeyacac, Juan saw as it were a white and shining cloud, and within it a rainbow of color, with rays of dazzling light. The Indian stood spellbound, yet unafraid, filled with a sweet amazement, and asked himself whether it were all a dream.

"What is this I hear and see? Where am I? By chance have I been transported to that Paradise of Delights where

11

our race came into being? Or is it some heavenly country, hidden from men's eyes?"

The singing was stilled, but the Indian remained in a kind of enchantment, gazing at the shining cloud above him on the hill. And then he heard a voice, a woman's voice, soft and clear, calling to him from the midst of the cloud: "Juan! Juan!"

Could he be hearing aright? Was the voice calling him?

There it came again, this time more sweetly insistent: "Juan! Come closer!"

Gone was all hesitation. Almost in a bound Juan Diego reached the little eminence and stood just below the shining cloud. And then Juan saw her! Within the shining cloud there stood a beautiful Lady. The radiance of her garments transformed into the likeness of precious jewels the stones beneath her feet, and the leaves of the hawthorn and nopal appeared clusters of rare emeralds on surfaces polished and glowing. The very soil had become a carpet of jasper, tinted in many colors.

"My son, Juan Diego, whom I love tenderly, like a small and delicate child! Where are you going?" The Lady's words were spoken in Nahuatl, the language of Juan's people. Who can reproduce their delicacy of feeling in any other tongue?

"O noble Mistress and my Lady," Juan answered, "I am going to Mexico, to the barrio of Tlaltelolco, to hear the Mass, which the ministers of God present for us in His place."

"Know, my well-beloved son," replied the Lady, "that I am the Ever-Virgin Mary, Mother of the true God, who is the Author of Life, the Creator of all things and the Lord of heaven and earth; who is everywhere. It is my wish that you build me a temple on this site. Here, as the loving Mother of you and of your fellow men, I will show forth my loving-kindness and compassion for your people and for those who love me and seek me, and call upon me in their labors and afflictions. Here I will hear their cries and their petitions, I will comfort and assuage. In order that my will may be accomplished, you must go to Mexico, to the palace of the Bishop who resides there. You are to tell him that I sent you, and that it is my pleasure that he build me a temple in this place. You will relate to him what you have seen and heard. And be certain of this: I will be grateful for what you do for me in this matter with which I charge you, and I will raise you up and make you renowned because of it. My son, you have heard my wish. Go in peace. And bear in mind that I will repay the labor and care that you employ; so in this matter exert all your strength."

On his knees and with head to the ground, Juan Diego answered: "I go, most noble Lady and my Mistress, as your humble slave, to carry out your order."

And so the Indian took leave of the Lady.

He descended the western slope of the hill and took the road into the City of Mexico, a league distant. As he had promised the Lady, Juan went directly to the palace of the Bishop, Fray Juan de Zumárraga. He asked the servants to tell the Bishop he wanted to see him; but, because of the early hour, and because they saw only an Indian of the poorest class, the servants simply let him wait. Finally, however, struck by his patience, they let him in, to audience with the prelate. On his knees before the Bishop, Juan poured out his story. Bishop Zumárraga listened to the extraordinary tale and questioned Juan closely. In the end he sent the Indian away, telling him to return in some days.

Sorrowfully Juan left the palace. The Bishop, he felt, had not believed the story. What was more important to Juan Diego, he had failed to carry out the will of the Blessed Lady. With heavy heart he began the journey to his pueblo, Tolpetlac.

It was after sunset when he reached the summit of Tepeyacac. The Lady was waiting for him. As soon as Juan saw her, he prostrated himself in obeisance and began to speak. But what other tongue can adequately convey the beauty and gentleness, the courtesy, the delicate nuances, of Juan Diego's native Nahuatl? Listen:

"My well-beloved Daughter, my Queen and Lady most high! I did what you commanded me, although I did not talk to the Bishop until after a long wait. I gave him your message in the form you commanded me; he heard me calmly and with attention. But, from what I observed in his manner, and from the questions which he put to me, I gathered that he did not believe me; for he told me to come back at a later date, so that he might investigate the matter at length. He thinks that the temple you wish to be built for you is a tale of my own making, or my own fancy rather than your will. So I pray you, for this work send some noble and important personage, worthy of respect, whom he will believe. For as you see, my Mistress, I am only a poor rustic, a lowly man of the people, and unsuited for this business on which you send me. Pardon my boldness, my Queen, if I have failed in the reverence due to your high station. Let not your wrath fall upon me, nor may my answer displease you."

The Most Holy Mary listened to his tale with a benign countenance, and then answered:

"Listen, my well-beloved son. Know you that I do not lack servants nor domestics under my command. For I have many whom I can send, if I wish, who will do what they are commanded. But it is fitting that you undertake this affair. It is through your intervention that my will and my desire must be done. So I ask you, my son, and I order you, to return tomorrow, to see and talk to the Bishop. Tell him to build me the temple that I ask, and tell him that she who sends you is the Virgin Mary, Mother of the true God."

"Do not be displeased, O Queen and my Lady," Juan Diego replied, "at what I have said. For I shall go willingly and with all my heart to obey your command and to carry your message. I was not making excuses, nor do I fear the journey nor the task. But perhaps I shall not be received nor listened to; or perhaps the Bishop, once he has heard me, will not believe. Nevertheless, I shall do what you command me. And I shall be waiting, Lady, tomorrow at sunset in this place, to give you the answer. And so remain in peace, and may God watch over you!"

Even through the dim medium of a translation twice removed from the original tongue, the delicacy of expression of this humble, unlettered man comes to us clearly, to our wonder and delight.

With reverence Juan Diego took his leave and continued on the way to his home in Tolpetlac. As far as we know, he said not a word to anyone about the matter. Perhaps, overcome by the events of the day and disturbed that the Bishop had not believed the tale, he had decided to keep his own counsel for the time being.

The next day, December the tenth, was Sunday, and Juan went to the Church of Santiago in Tlaltelolco for Mass and the class in Christian doctrine which the Indian converts had to attend. Then he went again to the palace of the Bishop. Once more the servants made him wait a long time, but finally he was admitted. Once more, prostrate and with tears and urgent words, Juan related to Bishop Zumárraga " . . . how for the second time he had seen the Mother of God in the same place that he had seen her the first time. That she was waiting for the reply to the message which she had given him earlier. That once again she had commanded him to go and tell the

Bishop to build her a temple on the very site where he had seen and talked to her. That he should tell the Bishop that she who sent him was the Mother of Jesus Christ and the Ever-Virgin Mary."

The Bishop listened with greater attention this time, and began to think that there might be something to the tale. He questioned and re-questioned Juan Diego very closely, warning him to weigh his words carefully. He asked Juan to describe the appearance of the Virgin, and satisfied himself that it could be neither dream nor imagination. Yet, as Bishop, he could not appear to accept lightly such a tale from the lips of a simple Indian. So he replied:

"What you have told me is not enough to make me undertake the task that you request. Therefore, tell the Lady who sent you to give you other signs, by which I may know that it is the Mother of God who sent you, and that it is her will that we build her a temple."

"What sign would you like me to ask for?" said Juan.

The calmness and confidence of Juan Diego strangely disturbed the Bishop. The Indian spoke as though the sign were as good as granted. And so the Bishop answered:

"Let the Lady choose whatever sign seems good to her."

Then he summoned several of the most trusted servants in his household. Speaking to them in Spanish, which Juan did not understand, the Bishop told them to follow Juan without his knowledge, to report upon what he did and with whom he spoke. The servants followed Juan, easily keeping him in sight until he arrived at a little bridge crossing a stream, almost at the foot of Tepeyacac. Here the Indian disappeared from their sight, and although the servants looked everywhere, searching the hill on every side, Juan could not be found. They took him for either an impostor or a wizard, and returned to tell the Bishop what had occurred, asking him to punish the Indian if he should again come to the palace.

When Juan reached the summit of the hill, the Virgin was waiting for him. On his knees he told her what had happened: "... how," as the most ancient recital has it, "carrying out her command, he had returned to the palace of the Bishop and had given him her message. And that, after questions and cross-questions, the Bishop had said that this simple tale was not sufficient to make him take action in so serious a matter."

Juan continued his relation:

"I am to ask you, O Lady, for a particular sign, by which he may know that you sent me, and that it is your will that a temple for you be built on this site."

With loving words Mary commended the care and diligence of Juan. She told him to return on the morrow, when she would give him a sign that the Bishop would believe. Juan promised to return, and took his leave of the Sovereign Lady.

But on the next day, Monday, December the eleventh, Juan was unable to keep his promise. Upon reaching his pueblo, he found that his uncle, Juan Bernardino, was seriously ill. The greater part of the day Juan spent in looking for a *curandero* (native medicine man) and when finally he found one, the latter's ministrations only made the sick man worse. Juan Bernardino requested his nephew to go early on Tuesday to the Convent of Santiago at Tlaltelolco, for a priest who would administer the last rites of the Church. Before daybreak on Tuesday, December the twelfth, therefore, Juan Diego set out for Tlaltelolco. But when he arrived at the foot of Tepeyacac, and was about to take the trail over the hill, he recalled his neglected promise to the Lady. Thinking that she would reproach him, he determined to avoid a meeting by skirting the hill. But as Juan approached the spot where today there is a spring of sparkling water, Mary came forth to meet him.

Encompassed by a shining cloud, she came down the hill, directly across his path, and spoke: 'Where are you going, my son, and what road are you taking?"

Struck with shame and fear, the Indian fell to the ground and answered:

"My beloved Daughter and my Lady, may God watch over you! Do not be displeased at what I am going to tell you. Know, my Mistress, that one of your servants, my uncle, is gravely ill and about to die, and as he seems very weak I am going to the temple of Tlaltelolco for a priest to confess and anoint him. After having discharged this duty I will return here to obey your command. Forgive me, I pray you, my Lady, and bear with me a little. I am not asking to be excused from doing what you have commanded, nor is it a false excuse I give you. Tomorrow I will return without fail."

Mary heard the Indian's story with understanding in her face, and then spoke to him in this manner:

"Listen, my son, to what I tell you now. Do not let anything worry or afflict you; do not fear illness nor any troublesome happening nor pain. Am I not here, I who am your Mother? Are you not under my shadow and protection? Am I not your life and health? Are you not in my embrace and in my prayers? What else do you need? Have no care nor worry about the illness of your uncle, for he will not die from it. Rest assured that he is already well."

Consoled by the words of Our Lady, Juan replied: "Then send me, my Lady, to see the Bishop, and give me the sign of which you spoke so that he will believe me."

And Mary answered: "My dearly beloved son, go up to the summit of the hill where you have seen me and talked with me, and cut the roses which you find there. Gather them into your cloak and bring them to me. I will tell you what you are to do and say."

Without another word Juan obeyed, although he knew that the rocky summit had never produced flowers, nor vegetation of any kind. But, arrived at the top, he found a beautiful garden of Castilian roses, fresh and fragrant and covered with dew. Laying out his *tilma* (mantle), he gathered into it as many roses as it would hold, and carried them to Mary. And Mary gathered up the roses and rearranged them in the mantle of Juan Diego, saying:

"You see here the sign which you are to take to the Bishop. Tell him, by the sign of these roses, to do what I order him. And pay attention, my son, to what I am telling you, and know that I have confidence in you. Show no one on the way what you are carrying, nor open your cloak except in the presence of the Bishop, and tell him what I sent you for. This will convince him that he is to start work on my temple."

And so saying, the Virgin sent him away.

At the episcopal palace, Juan Diego asked to see Bishop Zumárraga; but as before, the retainers saw only a humble Indian, and paid him little attention. Finally someone became curious about what he was carrying so carefully in his *tilma*, but Juan refused to show them. With some force they pulled at the cloak, and obtained a glimpse of the roses. At this discovery the retainers informed the Bishop, and Juan was brought into his presence. The Indian gave him Our Lady's message, and added that he had brought from her the sign which the Bishop had demanded. When he let fall the ends of his mantle, a shower of roses covered the floor, and upon his garment was seen the image of Our Lady, just as Juan had seen her on the hill of Tepeyacac. The astonished Bishop venerated the miraculous image before his entire household, and then bore it reverently to his private chapel.

Later, Juan was conducted, with signs of great respect, to the home of Juan Bernardino, by Spaniards who were commissioned to investigate the cure of the old man. Juan Bernardino related how the Most Holy Virgin had visited him at the very moment his nephew affirmed the cure had taken place, and had perfectly restored his health. The Virgin also told him " ... that it was her pleasure for a temple to be erected for her in the place where his nephew had seen her; and also that her sacred image was to be called *Santa María de Guadalupe.*"

Such is the simple tradition, told without embellishment. Why Our Lady called her image *Guadalupe* she did not say, nor shall we know, until she herself reveals it to us. At any rate, the title is not to be confused with that of the image of Our Lady of Guadalupe in Extremadura, Spain, said to have been sculptured by Saint Luke, and representing the Divine Maternity of the Blessed Virgin. Juan Bernardino, speaking the Nahuatl language, most probably called the Virgin *Xanta Malia Tecuauhtlanopeuh,* which signifies "Saint Mary, she who appeared on the rocky summit." What we do know is that the Virgin of Guadalupe united the tribes and races of Mexico into a nation, for all recognize her as their Mother. Of the million and a half Indians baptized by 1531, almost all had been among the poor and the children. The noble Aztec families, mindful of their former glory, had nourished resentment of the Spanish conquerors and their religion. But with the miracle of Guadalupe, class distinctions were put aside, and noble and commoner, landholder and peasant, cacique and tribesman, embraced the Faith. Six years after Tepeyacac there were nine million converts among the Indians, embracing the nucleus of all the nations among the tribes in the valley of Anáhuac. Mexico thus became the first Christian nation of the American continent.

The first little temple was finished, and the miraculous image placed therein on the twenty-sixth of December, 1531. This temporary structure was replaced by one of adobe, built at the expense of Bishop Zumárraga, and finished in 1533. The sacred image remained there until November, 1622, when Archbishop Juan de la Serna solemnly blessed a new collegiate church on the site. In 1895 the reconstruction of that edifice was completed for the Pontifical Coronation of the image of Our Lady of Guadalupe. In 1931 a further reconstruction was carried out, to commemorate the four-hundredth anniversary of the apparitions.

On the twelfth of October, 1895, Our Lady of Guadalupe was solemnly crowned, in the name of His Holiness Pope Leo XIII, as Queen of the Mexican People. And on the twenty-fourth of August, 1910, with the approbation of Pope Saint Pius X, the Virgin of Tepeyacac was named Celestial Patron of Latin America.

Those who are privileged to visit the basilica in the Villa de Guadalupe may see the original image which Our Lady presented to Juan Diego. This miraculous painting shows us the Virgin as we are accustomed to visualize her under her title of the Immaculate Conception. She appears as an Indian maiden of royal lineage, about fifteen years of age. Beneath her feet is a half-moon, resting upon the head of a cherub, who holds in the right hand the end of her mantle, and in the left the train of her tunic, which drapes in great folds about her feet. Her features are slightly darker than the color of a pearl, the lips a soft shade of red, the eyes modestly cast down. The hands are joined before the breast in an attitude of prayer, and the whole appearance is at once virginal and regal. The tunic, of a rosy tint, bears an idealized floral pattern in gold; it is closed at the neck with a yellow button bearing a cross of dark brown. At the waist the ends of a purple cincture may be seen just below the joined hands. The mantle is of blue-green, bordered with gold and oversown with golden stars regularly spaced, forty-six being visible. Upon the head, modestly inclined to the right, is a crown of ten golden rays. The Virgin appears to stand with the sun at her back, from which one hundred twenty-nine rays of gold shoot forth, alternately straight and serpentine. The rays terminate in an ashen-yellow background upon a field of red, forming a kind of niche for the image of Our Lady of Guadalupe.

It was before the image of Our Lady of Guadalupe, in Rome, that Pope Benedict XIV exclaimed: *"Non fecit taliter omni nationi,"* echoing the words of the One Hundred and Forty-seventh Psalm: "[S]he has not done thus for any other nation."

Perhaps we cannot better close this account of the most marvelous of Mary's wonders in Mexico than by using the words of the great Pontiff, Leo XIII: "Never before has it been given us on this earth to see so lovely an image; and its loving-kindness moves us to reflect: 'How beautiful must Mary herself be, in heaven!'"

OUR LADY OF SAINT-JOHN-OF-THE-LAKES

San Juan de los Lagos, Jalisco

III

NUESTRA SEÑORA DE SAN JUAN DE LOS LAGOS

(OUR LADY OF SAINT-JOHN-OF-THE-LAKES)

San Juan de los Lagos, Jalisco

𝒯ODAY San Juan de los Lagos is a large and thriving town, but in the year 1623 it was a collection of grass-roofed mud huts called *San Juan Bautista Mezquititlán,* inhabited by Indians of the Nochiztleca tribe. Their devotion was centered about an image of Our Lady of the Immaculate Conception, made of Michoacán clay, and considerably damaged by the elements. Very likely the saintly Franciscan missioner, Fray Miguel de Bolonia, had brought it to Mezquititlán many years before. The image was housed in a *zacate-*roofed chapel some fifty feet by twelve, in the care of an old Indian, Pedro Antes, and his wife Ana Lucía, a woman of seventy-eight years.

The devotion of Ana Lucía to the Virgin was well known in the pueblo, and she related many marvelous stories of her conversations with *La Virgencita.* Still, the Holy Office of the Inquisition, although ever vigilant to promote the spread of true devotion and to put down superstitious practices, did not bother to take any depositions from Ana Lucía, judging her tales to be the hallucinations of a senile woman. So the image remained neglected. It had even been removed from its former place of honor over the altar to a corner of the sacristy,

23

with scarcely anyone except Ana Lucía to look upon its blackened and disfigured features. Then in 1623, according to early legends, something occurred to reanimate and spread devotion to Our Lady.

It appears that a certain *volatín* (aerial acrobat) was traveling along the *camino real* (king's highway) from San Luis Potosí to Guadalajara, giving performances in the wayside towns. Together with his wife and two daughters, he would fly through the air between fixed points by means of ropes, in somewhat the manner of the trapeze artists of our day. To give the added thrill of danger to the act, the performers had to fly over swords and daggers, fixed in the ground point upward.

Shortly after they reached Mezquititlán, the younger daughter, a child of six or seven years, in the course of practicing for the performance, fell upon the knives and was fatally wounded. The grieving parents brought her body to the chapel of Our Lady of San Juan for burial.

Old Ana Lucía, the caretaker's wife, touched by the sorrowful spectacle, approached the dead child with the image of the Virgin. She exhorted the parents to have confidence in the designs of the Almighty: the *Cihuapilli* ("Lady") would bring the child back to life. Then she laid the statue upon the little corpse. In a few moments the body could be seen to move under the burial clothes. Quickly the parents cut the bonds of the burial shroud, and the child sat up, well and unharmed. From this time on, the miracles and favors reportedly gained through Our Lady of San Juan de los Lagos were numerous.

The grateful father asked that he be allowed to take the sacred image to Guadalajara to be restored and vested. The pastor, Don Diego Camarena, gave his permission, and directed certain Indians to accompany him and bring back the statue. When they arrived in the city, a man approached them. Were they looking for an artist to repair a sacred image? If so, he was at their service. They agreed with him on a price, and he took the statue away. Shortly afterward, it was returned to them with the face and hands beautifully finished. No one ever learned the identity of the mysterious artisan, it is said.

As the miracles attributed to Our Lady of San Juan multiplied, devotion to her image spread. In 1631 a new sanctuary was constructed, enclosing within its walls the primitive shrine. Today this edifice is the parochial church. In later years, the sanctuary could not accommodate the multitudes of the Virgin's clients who came from all parts of Mexico for feasts and pilgrimages. On the thirtieth of November, 1732, the first stone was laid for a magnificent temple to Our Lady, with its own collegiate chapter of canons to sing the Divine Office of the Church each day. In 1926 a Papal Bull of Pope Pius XI erected the temple into a collegiate church.

Not the least of the glories of Our Lady of San Juan de los Lagos occurred on August the fifteenth, 1904. On that day Don José Jesús Ortiz, Archbishop of Guadalajara, solemnly crowned the miraculous image. The permission of the Holy See, which authorized the liturgical crowning of Our Lady of San Juan de los Lagos, was granted by His Holiness Pope Saint Pius X. The authorization took into account the following facts:

(1) the antiquity of the venerable image;
(2) the great popularity of devotion to Our Lady of San Juan de los Lagos;
(3) the abundance of miracles attributed to Mary's intercession through the sacred image.

Devotion to Our Lady of San Juan is widespread today. The popular feast at her shrine is December 15, the Octave

of the Feast of the Immaculate Conception. Notwithstanding
the distance, the inconvenience of getting to San Juan de los
Lagos, and the shortage of accommodations there, Mary's de-
votees come from such faraway places as Mexico City, Puebla,
San Luis Potosí, Guanajuato — some even from the United
States.

The image is sculptured, the material of which it is formed
being *pasta de Michoacán,* a combination of cornstalks and
glue. In spite of the nature of this substance, which has little
durability and commonly crumbles to pieces in a relatively
short time, the sacred image has remained whole and unmarked
during the three and one-half centuries of its existence. The
figure is very small, measuring about a foot in height. The face
is somewhat aquiline, the eyes large, widely spaced, and dark
in color. The hands are joined, the fingers slightly separated.

The crown is of gold, in the Byzantine style with some
modifications. It is some seven inches high and weighs six
pounds. The crown contains 197 precious stones, including
diamonds, emeralds, and sapphires. Above the image are two
angels of silver, supporting between them a silver banner with
the inscription in blue enamel: *Mater Immaculata, ora pro
nobis.*

On July 14, 1678, Don Juan Santiago de Garabito,
twentieth Bishop of Guadalajara, directed the *Bachiller* Nicolás
de Arévalo, in writing, to "ascertain the miracles worked
through Our Lady of San Juan from the eighteenth of March
of 1668; the devotion which it enjoys; whether it is a painting
or a sculpture and of what size; its distance from the Villa of
Lagos and from Guadalajara; the gifts which have been given
to it; the ornaments, decoration of the sanctuary, condition of
the temple, and the year in which it was last renovated, with
the ornamentation of the towers." In other words, the Bishop
wanted to know anything that might relate to the image. To

the detailed reply of Nicolás de Arévalo we are indebted for much interesting information about the image and its sanctuary.

The image is undoubtedly a representation of the Immaculate Conception. In fact, while it was at first called "Our Lady of San Juan" by reason of the pueblo in which the statue was venerated, the official name in the confraternity, erected later, was "Our Lady of the Conception in the Pueblo of San Juan."

The principal feast is December the eighth, the Feast of the Immaculate Conception. It is traditionally celebrated with great solemnity. Here is a glimpse from an eyewitness account of the feast in the seventeenth century:

"On the seventh, Vespers is sung with the assistance of twenty or twenty-two priests who come from different parts. In the night, many fireworks are set off, and more than seventy festival pieces of wood are burned, and six hundred of paper, and many little rockets with fuses. The eighth is celebrated with Mass and a sermon. On the altar they burn a hundred and fifty candles; one year it was two hundred. The Most Holy Virgin goes out in procession on her silver litter, carried on the shoulders of priests, and under a canopy of white wool flecked with gold. The procession is through the cemetery, which alone has sufficient space.

"That evening they place on the altar two small vases of silver, one with twelve or fourteen papers with the names of devotees of this Lady, and the other with a like number of papers, all blank save one which reads 'Feast of Our Lady of San Juan.' One paper at a time is drawn from each vase, and the devotee who draws the paper which says 'Fiesta' is the one who has the honor of making the drawing the following year: an honor highly coveted and sought after. At this point the bells are rung and the guns fired. After the drawing, the Most Holy Virgin is taken down for the public to kiss, and if by the hour of prayer they have not finished,

because of the crowd, they come back to kiss the image the
following day."

Padre Francisco de Florencia, who wrote of Our Lady of
San Juan in the eighteenth century, tells us that the Virgin
Mary shows her face in images to remind us that we must
raise our eyes beyond them to her whom our faith recognizes,
and whom our will venerates, in each material representation.
And therefore, those who have the good fortune to visit
Nuestra Señora de San Juan piously ask Our Lady for the
grace to see her features in heaven.

OUR LADY OF COMPASSION
Mexico, D. F.

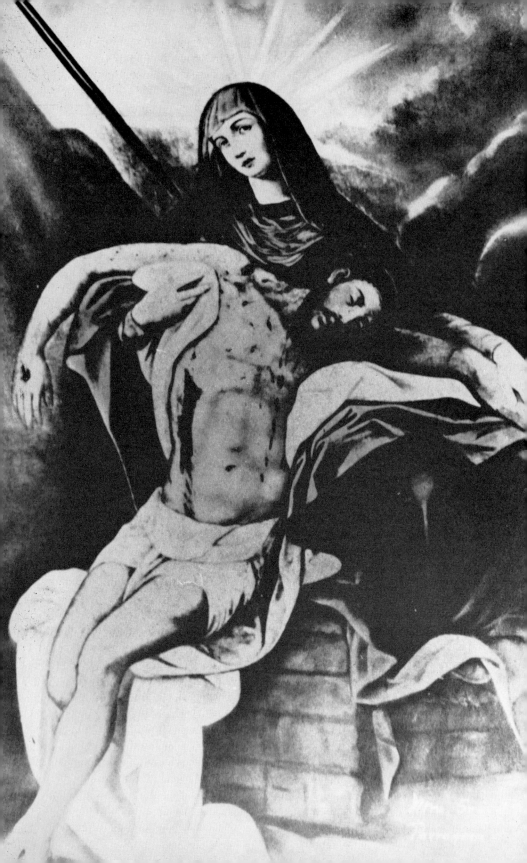

IV

NUESTRA SEÑORA DE LA PIEDAD

(OUR LADY OF COMPASSION)

Mexico, D. F.

*T*HE Convent of Our Lady of La Piedad dates back to the year 1595. Don Luis de Velasco II, when he was Viceroy of New Spain, had as his confessor a Dominican, Fray Cristobal de Ortega, who also acted as his financial adviser. In gratitude for the friar's diligence and loyalty to his interests for many years, Don Luis presented the Dominican Order with the convent on the twelfth of March, 1595.

Shortly afterward, a Dominican religious, accompanied by a Lay Brother, had to go to Rome on business for the Order. The religious of the new Convent of La Piedad commissioned him to bring back a painting of Our Lady under her title of *La Piedad* that is, "Compassion," representing the sorrowing Mother holding in her arms the lifeless body of her Divine Son. Rome in that day was the home of many outstanding painters, and the friar was charged with securing the best possible work of art.

On arrival, as an old legend relates, the religious asked an artist of great merit to accept the commission. The painter agreed, but would not set a date upon which he would undertake to have the picture ready. In vain the friar tried to fix the time, saying that he had to return to Mexico very soon,

29

and could not leave without the painting. But the artist only replied that he could not promise it by any definite date, since he worked only when inspiration came to him.

Finally, when they came to an agreement on the conditions under which the artist would accept the assignment, the Dominican began to describe the general outlines of the picture he wanted. Brusquely the artist cut him short. He knew his business; all the good friar had to do was wait. When the painting was ready, he would be notified.

The Dominican left the studio with mixed emotions. He had secured the artist's promise, true. On the other hand, the great man had shown very little interest in the project.

Time went by, and no word came from the artist. Very soon the religious would have to return to Mexico. Finally he could wait no longer. With some misgivings he visited the studio. Had the painting been finished?

"Finished?" answered the artist, with haughty indifference. "Why, I have scarcely begun to make a sketch of it!"

The poor friar did not know what to do. His superiors had ordered him to leave for New Spain the following morning. For some time he stood in thought, and at last he said:

"I will take back the sketch, at least, so that they may see it is no fault of mine."

"And what good will a simple sketch do?" asked the painter.

"In Mexico, we shall find someone who can finish the painting."

"Only one brush can complete this picture," replied the painter; "mine!"

"But I mean, with the help of God!" burst out the friar.

These words, uttered with such simple faith, shook the artist from his indifference — something that even a bag of gold pieces would not do — and he handed over the sketch.

A month later, the friar and his Lay Brother companion were in mid-ocean, bound for New Spain. Suddenly a storm arose, the like of which in ferocity and intensity the crew and passengers had never before experienced.

"*Padre!* We shall be drowned!" they cried in terror.

"Have confidence in Our Lady, Star of the Sea," the priest answered serenely. "She can calm the waters with a glance."

"We will promise her a thank-offering if she spares our lives," they said.

"Then let us make a promise to Our Lady," replied the friar, "to build her a sanctuary in Mexico." And so they promised.

At once the storm began to subside, and soon the sea was calm again. The grateful crew and passengers, mindful of their promise, made generous offerings.

Shortly thereafter the ship arrived at Veracruz, and the two Dominicans made their way overland to Mexico City. Their fellow religious at the Convent of La Piedad were considerably chagrined to learn the inconsequential outcome of the friar's business with the Roman artist. Some complained that they might have secured a suitable painting in Mexico, for a fraction of the cost, and much more quickly. Others said it might be a chastisement from God for their vanity in choosing a famous artist to do the work. With many misgivings, they set about opening the crate in which the sketch had crossed the ocean. As they were unrolling the canvas, signs of color were seen, but they assumed that some paint had adhered to it in the artist's studio. Their astonishment increased as they continued unwrapping the canvas, and when it was exposed to view, they gazed at it in silence, unable to take their eyes from the painting. For painting it was, of extraordinary beauty and perfection, depicting the Mother of Jesus holding her crucified Son.

"No doubt our brother sought to surprise us," said one.

"But he would not tell a falsehood for that," replied others.

So absorbed were they in the painting that it was some time before they saw that the two newly returned religious were still on their knees before the picture, overcome by the marvelous outcome of events. When they were at last able to speak, they related the circumstances in which they had acquired a rough sketch for the painting. They added the tale of the storm at sea and the near-shipwreck. They told how the crew and passengers had come to them with the promise to build a shrine for the Virgin if she spared their lives. When they had concluded their recital, all agreed that the hand of God had played a part in the supernatural affair of the painting. So runs the pious tradition.

From that time the religious of the Convent of La Piedad preached devotion to Our Lady in her image. Notable miracles have been worked through her intercession, and many of the most outstanding have been certified by formal process before the ecclesiastical tribunal.

This venerable image today hangs in the new sanctuary of Our Lady of La Piedad. It is an oil painting on canvas nearly nine feet high and eight and a half feet in width, in a wood frame, today covered with glass. The picture symbolizes the supreme moment when the Son of God, having enacted the drama of Calvary, lay in the arms of His Mother. A soft, clear light illumines the whole, and the colors are as fresh and bright as though the scene had been painted yesterday, instead of more than three and a half centuries ago.

Many indulgences have been granted to the Church of La Piedad, and it has been erected into a Minor Basilica.

OUR LADY OF HOLY HOPE
Jacona, Michoacán

V
NUESTRA SEÑORA DE LA ESPERANZA

(OUR LADY OF HOLY HOPE)

Jacona, Michoacán

OWARD the end of the seventeenth century (about 1685), dates the appearance, upon the waters of the Lake of Chapala, of a remarkable image of the Blessed Virgin Mary. An early chronicler, Father Mathías de Escobar of the Augustinian Order, writing in 1729, speaks of marvelous signs in the heavens, and two great stars which appeared.

At this time, tradition relates, there lived in the pueblo of Jacona a humble Indian named Juan. Juan was the godfather of another Indian from the pueblo of Pajacuarán, not far away, and at times Juan aided his godson, who was a fisherman, to ply his trade on the waters of the great Lake of Chapala. One day, while they were on the lake, they saw a huge tree root bobbing up and down in the water. Moved by a common impulse, they left off fishing, drew the root into their boat, and brought it ashore. The fisherman took it to his hut with the idea of drying it out for firewood. Several days later, when the sun had dried it sufficiently, he began to make a fire with it. At that moment Juan of Jacona arrived for another day of fishing. When he entered the hut, his attention was drawn to the great root, wherein he perceived the outlines of an image of the Virgin. Juan begged his godson

for the root, and the other granted the request. Forgetful now
of fishing, Juan shouldered the heavy piece of wood and made
his way back to Jacona. Once within his own poor dwelling,
he saw that he had not been mistaken, for the root, from a
tree which the Indians call *camichin,* indeed formed a marvelously perfect likeness of the Virgin Mary holding her Divine
Son.

The sacred image, together with its golden pedestal,
measures scarcely forty inches in height. It has a beauty and
grace that is neither ancient nor modern in feeling. Unlike
the typically Spanish images of the Virgin, with a widespread
mantle over a pink or rose tunic, *La Esperanza* wears the white
tunic made for her coronation, and a tastefully ornamented
blue mantle gracefully falling in a natural line. Her right
heel rests upon the head of the "ancient serpent," and her right
arm encloses a bouquet of white lilies. Altogether it is a loving
representation of the Immaculate Conception, and manifests
those characteristics of our Heavenly Mother which inspired
Pope Pius IX to call her "Mother of Holy Hope."

Later hands, with an indiscreet zeal, have removed the
Divine Infant from the breast of His Mother. The same mistaken devotion did not allow the earlier devotees to leave the
features of the Virgin in the original natural color of the root.
Regrettably, they scraped and lacquered the features, partially destroying the natural marvels of the image. Yet even
today traces of the root can be seen on the head and on parts
of the figure.

Even if there were nothing remarkable in the origins of
this venerated image, it has another and possibly greater claim
to the devotion of Mary's children. For Our Lady of Holy
Hope is the first image in the Americas to be solemnly crowned.
The circumstances surrounding this fact merit our attention.

In April, 1885, the image of *La Madonna della Strada* was solemnly crowned in the Church of the Gesù in Rome. This image is venerated in the chapel where Saint Ignatius Loyola and his first companions were accustomed to celebrate Mass. At the time of the coronation a young Mexican seminarian in Rome, Miguel Plancarte, was awaiting ordination to the sub-diaconate at the Colegio Pio Latino-Americano. In all his years at the Colegio, it was the only coronation that young Plancarte had witnessed. The magnificence of the ceremony greatly impressed him, and on that occasion he formed the idea of obtaining the honor of a like coronation for the Virgin of Guadalupe, Patroness of Mexico. But there was a difficulty. The basilica of Guadalupe had a Cathedral Chapter, and what with the conflicting opinions of its canons, and his own wholly unofficial position, Plancarte realized that to attain his goal would be virtually impossible at that time. So he determined to set himself an easier, if nonetheless considerable, task. He would secure from the Pope permission to crown *La Esperanza,* the image to which he had great devotion from childhood, in his native Diocese of Zamora. Once crowned, *La Esperanza* would serve to stimulate the devotion of his countrymen and to pave the way for the coronation, not only of Our Lady of Guadalupe, but of all the images of the Virgin Mary in the most venerated shrines in Mexico and in the rest of America.

Paying no heed to the admonitions of his friend the chaplain at the shrine in Jacona, who feared that the young seminarian was attempting the unattainable, Plancarte went ahead. Secure in the conviction that the Blessed Virgin herself, "who had caught him in those brambles," as he writes, would without doubt free him from them, the enthusiastic cleric ordered a crown from Brago, the Vatican silversmith, and a set of royal robes from Tanfani, the pontifical vestment designer. Pope Leo XIII granted the petition, and by the end of Sep-

tember, 1885, Plancarte held in his hands a Papal Brief by
which the Pope authorized the coronation with a crown of
gold, in his own name, of the sacred image of Our Lady, dele-
gating the actual crowning to Archbishop Don Pelagio Antonio de Labastida y Dávalos. Moreover, His Holiness personally blessed the crown — an unusual favor.

When Miguel Plancarte left the Pio Latino on the fifteenth
of October, 1885, an ordained priest, he was carrying back to
Mexico the Papal Brief and the royal crown and vestments.
On the fourteenth of February, 1886, the Pontifical Coronation
of the Virgin of *La Esperanza* took place with the greatest
possible ceremony in the atrium of Mary's shrine in Jacona,
before sixteen thousand people crowded into the municipal
plaza. It was a superb manifestation of faith and love for the
Virgin Mary.

In the same year of 1886, the Archbishop of Mexico entrusted to the *Cura* of Jacona, Don Antonio Plancarte y Labastida, the collecting of material preliminary to crowning Our
Lady of Guadalupe as Queen of Mexico. The archbishops of
the country jointly petitioned Pope Leo XIII for that privilege,
which was granted. The actual coronation of the Virgin of
Guadalupe was deferred for some years, while the basilica
of Guadalupe was being enlarged and decorated. At last the
dream which *"Padre Miguelito"* first dreamed in Rome in 1885
while he was still a seminarian, became a reality, on the twelfth
of October, 1895, when Our Lady of Guadalupe was crowned
Patroness and Sovereign of Mexico.

OUR LADY OF THE REMEDIES
San Bartolo Naucalpán, Mexico

VI

NUESTRA SEÑORA DE LOS REMEDIOS

(OUR LADY OF THE REMEDIES)

San Bartolo Naucalpán, Mexico

*T*HERE are many images of the Virgin Mary venerated in New Spain under the title *Los Remedios,* but the subject of this chapter has a most unusual history. Brought to Mexico with Hernán Cortés, it witnessed his triumphant entry into the Aztec capital. In the *Noche Triste,* or "Sorrowful Night" of the eighth of July, 1520, when the Spaniards were fleeing for their lives across the Puente de la Mariscala, north of the city, the image was in the care of a soldier, Juan Rodríguez de Villafuerte. Unable, very likely, to carry it farther, he hid the statue, in its case, under some maguey plants. There it remained for many years, while the broad leaves of the maguey grew up and around it. In 1540 an Indian *cacique* (chief), Juan Cuautli, while out hunting, rediscovered it. A recent convert to the Faith, he venerated it in his house for several years. Today the image stands above the main altar in the sanctuary of Los Remedios, only yards from its place of discovery.

The Virgin of Los Remedios is a wood sculpture of the Madonna and Child, about eleven inches in height. It is polychromed over gilt on fire-hardened wood — what the Spaniards call *estofada,* a virtually lost art. Green, blue, red, and gold can still be seen in the sculpture. In the early seventeenth century the practice of vesting sacred images came into vogue, and in our own times the Virgin of Los Remedios, like most of the images in Mexico, is richly dressed in embroidered robes.

At one time Mother and Child possessed sixteen complete changes of vestments. According to the descriptions in the ancient list, each garment carefully itemized and described, they must have been worth a king's ransom. Time and the caresses of devoted Mexicans have partially obliterated the features of both Mother and Child, but some of the paint remains fresh after almost four hundred and fifty years.

In times of public calamity Our Lady of Los Remedios was carried to the cathedral, in procession, from her sanctuary at San Bartolo Naucalpán, fourteen kilometers (about eight and a half miles) northwest of the capital. Between 1576 and 1922, the year of the last procession, the image has traveled to the cathedral a total of seventy-five times, always amid great solemnity. Several of these pilgrimages deserve particular mention.

The pestilence of 1576-77 had caused over two thousand deaths. Whole towns were depopulated; *finca* and farm were untended and overgrown. The physicians of the *Hospital Real* tried in vain to identify the plague and to isolate its cause. In the spring of 1577, the Archbishop, Don Pedro Moya de Contreras, and the Viceroy, Don Martín Enriquez, determined to take the image of Los Remedios to the cathedral. There a novena was conducted invoking the intercession of Our Lady under her title "Health of the Sick." When the nine days of prayer ended and the image returned to her sanctuary in the beginning of April, the rains began and continued through November, purifying the air and bringing the plague to an end.

In the great drought of 1597, no rain had fallen until well into August. The Viceroy, Don Gaspar de Zuñiga y Acevedo, requested that the Virgin of Los Remedios be taken in procession to the cathedral. Scarcely had the procession left the sanctuary when the rain fell in torrents. It is related that the streets became veritable streams, so that the carriage in which the image was riding had to be lifted upon the shoulders of the attendants to make any progress. During the novena, the rain did not fail a single day, and the drought was effectively broken.

The drought of 1616, along with insupportable heat, brought an epidemic that turned the City of Mexico into a vast hospital, and the lack of provisions brought starvation as well. Once more Our Lady of Los Remedios was petitioned to come to the cathedral. Accompanied by an assemblage that stretched away for more than a league, the venerable image arrived on the eleventh of June. The rains began and continued in such abundance that the year 1616 was one of the most fertile in the history of New Spain.

It may surprise some to learn that Our Lady of Los Remedios holds a high military rank. There is a painting, of the year 1813, which shows her vested in the shoulder sash of a captain general, wearing a sword, and carrying the gold command baton. This circumstance has an unusual history.

When the troops of France invaded Spain in 1809, the image was brought from the sanctuary to Mexico City and placed for a certain period in each of the convents belonging to the various religious orders. The religious at the Convent of Saint Jerome, when they received the image, dressed Our Lady, and her Infant as well, in the insignia of a captain general of the Army of New Spain. The regalia became very popular, and the image remained vested in this manner for some time.

On the morning of the thirtieth of October, 1810, the insurgent Hidalgo and his troops were marching on Mexico
City. The Viceroy, Venegas, had detailed a bodyguard of
thirty lancers to the shrine of Los Remedios. Fearing, however,
that the image might fall into the hands of the insurgents,
who had committed all manner of atrocities, the Viceroy had it
conveyed to the cathedral. The following day, accompanied
by a great number of people, he went to visit the sacred image.
On his knees, the Viceroy placed in the hands of Our Lady his
own staff of office, begging her to keep the city from devasta-
tion. Hidalgo turned back virtually at the gates of the capital.

On the twenty-first of February, 1811, a splendid procession and review took place in Mexico City. Along the main
thoroughfare were drawn up in ranks the regiments of militia
of the city and the Battalions of Noblemen of Ferdinand VII,
"so that, by command, they might render to the sacred image
the military honors corresponding to the rank of captain
general."

The Feast of Our Lady of Los Remedios is celebrated with
great solemnity during the first eight days of September, and
thousands of devout pilgrims come to San Bartolo Naucalpán
from many parts of the country. Pilgrims travel many miles on
foot and by every means of conveyance, ancient and modern,
to spend the entire eight days at the shrine. Hundreds of
Mexican Indian families, most of them with small infants,
jam the courtyards; at night sleeping shoulder to shoulder and
head to toe on *petates* of woven grass, by day observing and
taking part in the traditional dances in the plaza, and attend-
ing the numerous Masses celebrated in honor of Our Lady of
Los Remedios. And, of course, nobody goes home without
standing in line at least once, to climb the flight of steps
behind the main altar and do homage to the image of their
beloved *"Virgencita."*

OUR LADY OF GUANAJUATO

Guanajuato, Guanajuato

OUR LADY OF GUANAJUATO

Guanajuato, Guanajuato

VII
NUESTRA SEÑORA DE GUANAJUATO

(OUR LADY OF GUANAJUATO)

Guanajuato, Guanajuato

THE venerable image of Our Lady of Guanajuato has been an object of religious devotion in the city of Guanajuato since 1557. But it has a history that goes back far beyond that date. In fact, the original image at the shrine was probably the most ancient among the many that have been venerated, not merely in Mexico, but in the entire Western Hemisphere!

Tradition says it was known in Spain in the seventh century, being venerated in the city of Santa Fé in Granada as early as the year 650. Upon the invasion of Spain by the Moors in 714, some devout Granadans concealed the image in a subterranean crypt; in this way it escaped desecration at infidel hands. Our Lady's statue remained in its hiding place for some eight and a half centuries. Its rediscovery, on the basis of ancient documents, is remarkable enough. What is more amazing is that the image was not completely destroyed by the dampness and lack of ventilation. Whether the present statue is the original of the tradition, or a sixteenth-century replacement, in actual fact, the wood shows hardly the slightest sign of deterioration even today.

The image came to light again toward the middle of the sixteenth century. Shortly thereafter, Philip II sent it as a gift

to the city of Guanajuato. Undoubtedly the Spanish monarch
was influenced by the tremendous flow of wealth from the
mines of Guanajuato into the coffers of the royal treasury.
The sacred image was committed for its journey to the care
of a certain Don Perafán de Rivera. When he was about three
leagues distant from Guanajuato, at a spot called Yerba Buena,
nightfall caused his party to halt. Not knowing the exact
location of the city, the travelers decided to let the image
show them the way. They placed it on a drum and lighted
two candles, beseeching Our Lady for a sign to show them
where they were. Shortly, some doves flew into the camp.
Rightly assuming that there was a village nearby, the men
released the doves at dawn, and following the direction taken
by the birds, arrived at Guanajuato.

The image was placed in the church connected with the
hospital of the Aztec Indians (later to become the Capilla del
Colegio del Estado), where it remained eight years. Later it
was moved to a new chapel which was to be its home for 131
years. In 1696, the Mother Church of Guanajuato was dedicated, and the statue, richly endowed with jewels, was taken
to its own magnificent chapel in the Gospel nave. There it
remained until 1814, when it was placed over the main altar.
In 1838, when the main sanctuary was reconstructed, a triptych
of altars was designed and the image of the Virgin enthroned
over the central one.

In 1907 the faithful devotees of Our Lady of Guanajuato
besought permission of Pope Saint Pius X for the solemn
coronation of the venerable image. In consideration of the
great antiquity of the statue, the deep and widespread devotion to Our Lady of Guanajuato, and the numerous miracles
attributed to her intercession, the saintly Pontiff granted the
request. The Pontifical Coronation of Our Lady of Guanajuato took place on the thirty-first of May, 1908.

The visitor to the shrine at Guanajuato, whether he be a devout worshiper or merely a spectator, cannot fail to note the calm majesty of the image. According to the legend, it has borne more than twelve hundred years of vicissitudes. It has endured through a score of wars. It has seen the banner of the infidel fly over Catholic Spain, and Christian knights leave for the Crusades and return. It led a kind of catacomb existence for some eight centuries, and then crossed the Atlantic in a little sailing vessel. Yet the image venerated today is in a perfect state of preservation. Carved out of one piece of wood, forty-six inches in height, Our Lady is represented with the Divine Infant on her left arm. The right hand holds a rose carved of wood. Both Mother and Child are richly vested in garments embroidered with pearls, diamonds, and other precious stones, covering the original mantles and cloaks carved in wood. Our Lady wears a golden crown encrusted with pearls, and beneath her feet is a half-moon of gold. For a space of time the Virgin held a rosary in the right hand, but for valid motives and with the permission of the Bishop, the rosary was removed. In its place the sacred image holds a golden scepter, fastened by a pin through the carven rose.

This ancient image is not called by any of the usual titles under which Mary's children are accustomed to invoke her. She is known simply as "Our Lady of Guanajuato." As far as one can determine, the artist who made the statue did not intend to portray any particular mystery or event in the life of the Mother of Jesus, but only to make a perfect image of the Virgin.

Our Lady of Guanajuato is invoked in times of drought. There are many extraordinary cases on record of plentiful rain, following a procession with the sacred image. The people of Guanajuato believe there is something miraculous in the way Our Lady answers their prayers for rain, even in the years of greatest drought in Mexico. Merely to carry the image in procession seems to assure them of plentiful rain. There are three cases worthy of mention on record before 1900, all well-documented. Each time, when the rainy season was far advanced without a drop of water having fallen, the people carried Our Lady of Guanajuato in procession. Each time, while the procession was going through the streets, rain began to fall in such abundance that the image had to be taken hastily into the nearest church. There it remained each time for the nine days of prayer, while the rain continued.

The principal feast is that of the Patronage of Our Lady, the second Sunday of November each year. Every *guanajuatense* shares in the celebration, and class differences are forgotten as mineowner and humble *minero* join in honoring their venerable Patroness. Solemn Masses are sung in the churches crowded to the doors. Bands of *romeros* throng into the city from mountain villages and faraway cities. On the secular side, *cohetes,* church bells, and bands of musicians strive to outdo one another in raising the sound volume to previously unrecorded decibels. Homes, churches, and shops are decked in gaily colored bunting and strings of lights. Far into the night, the rockets and multicolored *castillos* manifest the general spirit of rejoicing and thankfulness with which the citizens of Guanajuato celebrate the Feast of their Patroness and Mother, Our Lady of Guanajuato.

OUR LADY OF THE ASSUMPTION
Tecaxic, Mexico

VIII

NUESTRA SEÑORA DE LOS ANGELES DE TECAXIC

(OUR LADY OF THE ASSUMPTION)

Tecaxic, Mexico

TWO miles west of Toluca on the road to Ixtapan de la Sal, and upward of half a mile in a northerly direction along a rocky unpaved road, barely negotiable by car in the dry season, stands the hamlet of Tecaxic. Its barren, rocky soil yields a grudging subsistence to the handful of native families whose huts of adobe make up the community. The name itself, from the Nahuatl *tecaxitl* (place of rocks), hints at the desolate character of the place. Yet, inconvenient of approach and desolate though Tecaxic may be, the devout traveler will be more than repaid for the sacrifices which his journey may entail. For it was precisely here that a deep and marvelous devotion to the Mother of God originated, having as its visible center a remarkable painting of the Assumption of Our Blessed Lady.

The origin of the sacred image is shrouded in the mists of Mexico's Catholic past, but it has been venerated for more than four hundred years. Like the Blessed Virgin of Guadalupe, Our Lady of the Angels is painted upon a *tilma* (native cloak) of cotton. Like the Guadalupe, too, the image is painted right through the material, so that it appears perfectly delineated in reverse, upon the back of the *tilma* as well!

45

The features are of remarkable beauty and sweetness. By some mastery of the artist, the Virgin appears to smile when one views her from the Epistle side of the church nave, and to exhibit a maternal sorrow in her glance when seen from the Gospel side.

Our Lady is depicted with her face slightly inclined to the right, but with no elevation or perspective, so that her gaze appears to follow one in every direction. The hair, which appears almost blond, is gracefully parted, with that on her right side falling forward over the shoulder, and that on the left behind the shoulder. The left ear is uncovered as if to assure her devoted children that Mary is ever ready to listen to their prayers and to help them in their needs.

The Virgin's hands are joined before her breast. The tunic is of purple; and the mantle of blue, star-studded, is held up and outward by four angels. A white stock covers the sacred figure from the throat to the junction of the tunic below the neck. The entire figure is enclosed within a flaming sun from which blaze forth rays of gold, breaking through the carmine-tipped snow clouds of the heavens. Above the head of the Virgin, between clouds and golden rays, God the Father, with a crown of gold in His hands, prepares to place it upon the Mother of His Son, to crown her Queen of Heaven.

Later hands have added a crown of gold, pearls, and precious stones, which has been attached to the surface of the painting and rests upon the head of the Virgin. The effect is by no means incongruous. The lower part of the painting shows a sepulcher with a casket of jasper, over which is draped a white stole. The Apostles and the holy women are ranged about the sepulcher looking upward. Two Apostles, perhaps Peter and John, with their hands placed upon an edge of the casket, gaze into it. The Virgin, accompanied by angels, is being carried up into heaven. Under her feet is a half-moon which rests upon the head of a cherub.

In early times, Tecaxic was a thriving pueblo, which had received the Faith through the preaching of the Franciscans from the convent in Toluca. But around the year 1640, a great plague practically wiped out the population. The only two surviving inhabitants fled, and for some time the pueblo was deserted.

Along with a few miserable Indian huts, there remained a tiny hermitage, with a small niche enclosed by two doors. Within this niche was hung an image of Our Lady of the Assumption, painted in distemper, upon a simple cloak of cotton, which is the native dress of the region. When the plague depopulated the village, the chapel fell into disrepair. In fact, the building became a complete ruin. The fierce storms of the rainy season broke the roof and the doors, tore gaping holes in the walls, and altogether so damaged the structure that the sacred image was left unsheltered, at the mercy of the elements. The summer rains drenched it. The burning sun scorched its fabric. The storms of dust brought by the hurricanes were more than enough to efface its lineaments.

The story of Father Antonio de Samano y Ledesma, a priest of that time, bears this out. One day, he writes, returning to his house, about two miles from Tecaxic, he was caught in a sudden rainstorm near the shrine. He decided to take shelter in it, but upon entering, he could not find a spot where the rain was less fierce than outside, and so continued on his way.

Yet by the almighty designs of Providence, the painting remains preserved. The colors are fresh and vivid, not only in the features of the Virgin, but even in the fine details of her garments. Drenched by the rains, battered by the winds, was this sacred image; yet its beauty remains unimpaired. It would almost seem as if the elements had conspired to beautify the features and refine its coloring, so as to prepare it for the great veneration which today the Virgin of Tecaxic enjoys.

It is even more noteworthy when one considers the weakness of the canvas, a coarse cotton of native weave, and the nature of the paint, distemper, which can ordinarily be smeared by rubbing. Add to these facts the circumstance that the image was thus exposed to the weather for years beyond the memory of the oldest inhabitants, many of whom testified that the chapel had been a complete ruin from their earliest childhood!

There are many remarkable local legends both in connection with the building of the sanctuary and devotion to the sacred image of the Virgin. The two which we narrate here are among a number documented by Fray Baltazar de Medina, Censor for the Holy Office of the Inquisition in the year 1684, on the testimony of reliable witnesses.

On one occasion a woman from the pueblo of Sinacantepec came on foot to visit the Virgin of Tecaxic. Of a race accustomed to bear suffering with stoicism, she was crying with pain from a cancerous arm, which was to be amputated the following day. Recommending herself to the Holy Virgin, and trusting with a lively faith in the compassion of the Queen of Heaven, she scraped some dust and earth which clung to the frame of the painting, mixed it with saliva, and formed a kind of mud which she applied to the diseased arm. She then returned to her house. The next day the surgeon, Cristobal Mejía, arrived to remove the arm. To his amazement he found it completely healed, without any mark or lesion. Both the patient and the surgeon attributed the miracle to Our Lady of the Angels.

On another occasion, an Indian woman from the pueblo of Calimaya, totally blind, came to the shrine of Our Lady, guided by a boy. She remained there nine days in prayer to the Virgin. On the road back to Calimaya, still guided by the youth, she suddenly found that she could see clearly. The woman returned to Tecaxic to give thanks to Our Lady, and related the story to Francisco de Fuentes, who preserved it for posterity.

Four men once came to Tecaxic from the pueblo of Comalco, carrying a woman between them on an *ayate* (grass mat). The poor creature was crippled in her hands and feet, unable to help herself. On a Thursday morning she was carried into the church to ask the intercession of Our Lady. On Saturday morning she walked out, well and strong, from the pilgrim shelter where she had spent the night, and entered the church to give thanks for her recovery. This remarkable cure was witnessed by a number of people.

Saint John Damascene, in relating the ancient tradition of the Assumption of the Blessed Virgin, writes of angelic music heard by the Apostles during the entombment of Mary in Gethsemani, and for three days thereafter. There is a mystical similarity between this sacred tradition and one which is told about the image of Our Lady of the Assumption of Tecaxic.

In the valley of Toluca lived Pedro Millan Hidalgo, a highly respected native of Toluca, who had retired to the pueblo of Almoyola, about two leagues away. His business took him in the evenings to Toluca, and the road led through Tecaxic, past the ancient sanctuary of Our Lady of the Angels. Often while passing the little chapel, especially on Wednesdays and Saturdays, he heard strains of music of such beauty as to excite his admiration. Sometimes, having gone a distance past the chapel, he felt compelled to turn back and see who the singers were. But upon entering the little shrine, he would find only silence and solitude. On other nights he would see, from a distance, the chapel resplendent with lights, and when he cautiously approached, find all in darkness.

The first night that he saw the lights, Pedro thought that the Indians of the Tecaxic pueblo were conducting a burial service. He had seen a dead man earlier in the day, and assumed that they were burying him at night and in a hidden place to evade the death fees to the convent of Toluca, under whose province the spiritual matters of Tecaxic came. The lights, of course, would have been candles lighted for the burial. Thus ruminating, Pedro arrived at the place, whereupon the lights were suddenly extinguished. Nor could he hear anyone within. Pedro presumed that the Indians had heard him coming, and had put out the candles and hidden themselves in the chapel, so as not to be caught in the act of interring a corpse without benefit of Christian burial. He entered the darkened chapel and began to speak in the Indian dialect.

"Don't be afraid, my sons — it is Pedro Millan."

But as they did not answer, and the chapel was dark, he unsheathed his sword and went about the little hermitage, prodding the walls and floor with the point of his weapon. The chapel was empty, save for Pedro himself! Full of a holy awe and reverence for the sacred image of the Virgin there, to whom he attributed the marvelous occurrence, he began the practice of burning a candle at the shrine each Saturday.

Pedro related to some of his friends the marvel of the music and the lights, and as all knew him for a truthful man, they believed his tale. Some out of curiosity, and others out of devotion, went at night to the shrine. Some claimed to have witnessed the lights and the music; others neither saw nor heard anything unusual.

News of these events spread throughout the valley of Toluca, into the city and its surrounding pueblos, and there sprang up a great devotion to Our Lady. In 1650 Fray José Gutiérrez, Guardian of the Convent of San Francisco in Toluca, began to build a new sanctuary, begging alms in Toluca and its environs. The devotion of the Indians was so great that many of them brought wood, lime, and other materials, and women and children even offered their labor without pay, being content with a bit of food each day. Today a diocesan parish the sanctuary is a monument of the love and devotion of many generations to the miraculous Virgin of Tecaxic.

IX

NUESTRA SEÑORA DE LOS ANGELES

(OUR LADY OF THE ANGELS)

Mexico, D. F.

IN THE year 1580, unprecedented rains flooded the valley of Mexico. The great lakes of Zumpango, Texcoco, and San Cristobal were insufficient to contain the waters, which broke through the dikes and swept down upon the Mexican capital. Streets became rivers, and homes were swept away. Especially in the outlying districts — the Indian barrios — where building materials were usually reed-cane and adobe, the destruction was great.

Among the flotsam carried by the flood was a beautiful depiction of the Virgin Mary on canvas, which finally came to rest in the barrio of Coatlán, or "place of saltpeter." In ancient times this had been the section reserved for the homes of the Toltec nobility. Under the Spanish law, this section was restricted to the Indian population, and no Spaniard could reside or own property there without permission.

In Coatlán lived an Indian *cacique* named Isayoque, a descendant of the Aztec nobility. The image of the Virgin came into his hands, and struck by its beauty, he built a small adobe chapel, or *santocalli,* where it might be kept for veneration. But dampness and maltreatment by the elements caused the paint to flake off, the canvas to rot, and the image

Es copia fi
de su ori
fLuis fa
año de

OUR LADY OF THE ANGELS
Mexico, D. F.

to lose much of its beauty. Isayoque by this time had conceived a great devotion to the image. He commissioned artists to make a faithful copy upon the adobe wall of the chapel. This is the image venerated today as "Our Lady of the Angels," in the Jesuit church of the same name built on the site of Isayoque's chapel, about a mile north of the Alameda.

We do not know the exact date that Isayoque built the adobe chapel. It is certain, however, that in 1595 it was officially constituted a public chapel by the Church authorities, and from then on used for public worship. The painting for many years was known as "The Assumption of Isayoque." Later, when the name of the *cacique* had faded from public memory in Coatlán, the image was called "Our Lady of the Angels." From 1595 the chapel was under the jurisdiction of the Church of Santiago in Tlaltelolco.

Gradually, devotion to the image weakened and virtually disappeared. The adobe chapel fell into ruins; its ceiling and all the walls, save the one containing the sacred painting, fell down, leaving the image exposed to the elements. How long it would have remained in this sorry state we do not know, but for the flood of 1607. Again the waters inundated Coatlán, and its inhabitants, in their affliction, turned their eyes once more to the image in the ruined chapel, so long neglected. They began to rebuild the chapel, forming a confraternity in honor of the Blessed Virgin for the construction and decoration.

Rebuilt in 1607 after the flood of that year, the chapel was maintained during the lifetime of the original members of the confraternity. Soon after, it fell again into ruins, with only the wall containing the sacred image left unharmed. In this condition it was the nightly shelter of a sheepherder and his flock. Abortive attempts to rebuild it were made in 1737 and again in 1744. Then, by order of the Archbishop of Mexico, because of numerous abuses, the authorities forbade

veneration of the image, and in 1746, sealed it behind grass
mats and boards nailed into the adobe. This should have been
more than enough to damage the painting considerably, if not
to destroy it altogether.

But in 1747, the Inquisitor Don Pedro Navarro de Isla
removed the mats and boards and found the image undam-
aged! There is a record in 1764 of two priests, Don José
Benito de Alvarado and Don Agustín Anastasio Navarro, asking permission to celebrate Masses there. However, little by
little the chapel was falling into decay, and in 1776 we know
that it was a complete ruin.

And now for a happier period in the existence of Our
Lady of the Angels. It began on the twenty-eighth of February, 1776. On that day, José de Haro, a master tailor, was
being driven to the Colegio of Santiago Tlaltelolco, to measure
one of the students for a new suit. Passing by the ruined
shrine, he stopped the coach. Through the mass of shapeless
adobe and sagging beams, the sunlight fell upon the features
of Our Lady of the Angels. Struck by the sight of the image
in such sordid surroundings, he resolved to preserve it and to
restore the chapel. With his own funds and the assistance of
some generous friends, and with the permission of the Archbishop of Mexico, he began the renovation of the sanctuary.
Soon a chapel of considerable proportions had been completed.
José de Haro was named custodian *in perpetuum* of the shrine,
and he held this office until 1790, when at his own request,
by reason of advanced age, he was relieved of the task of love
to which he had devoted so many years.

In 1793, Pope Pius VI affiliated this Church of Our Lady
of the Angels with the Church of Saint John Lateran in Rome,
and conceded to Our Lady's sanctuary, in virtue of that aggre-
gation, all the Indulgences to be gained in a Lateran church.
Pope Gregory XVI granted its own special Office in the Roman

Breviary to the *cultus* of Our Lady of the Angels. The saintly Pope Pius IX granted to the sanctuary the Jubilee of the Portiuncula, with all its accompanying Indulgences.

Finally, under the guardianship of the Fathers of the Society of Jesus, who now have the care of the church, the Pontifical Coronation of Our Lady of the Angels took place. On the twenty-eighth of October, 1923, in the name of Pope Pius XI, the sacred image was crowned by Archbishop Don José Mora y del Rio. Thus "crowned, she triumphs forever," living in the hearts of her beloved people.

To recount the marvels worked through the intercession of *Nuestra Señora de los Angeles* would require a volume in itself. We shall content ourselves with the mention of only two or three among the thousands of well-documented favors granted by Our Lady.

Fray Pablo Patiño, Vice-Commissar of the Holy Land, who wrote a notable dissertation upon Our Lady of the Angels, published the following account of a favor granted to himself:

"I affirm that I owe to the Most Holy Queen of the Angels the singular favor of having been freed from a raging fever. The physicians of this city [Mexico] had despaired of my life. I was experiencing the final attacks and the accompanying agony. A garment of Our Lady was placed over me and then the fever began to diminish, so that within an hour the beneficial effect was noticeable. The sickness passed its crisis at the very moment when the vestment was applied to me. I should be ungrateful if I did not make it known."

Another remarkable and widely published cure attributed to Our Lady of the Angels is connected with Pope Pius IX. Dr. Don José Santiago, chaplain of the sanctuary of Nuestra Señora de los Angeles, treasured a copy of the image painted on the adobe wall of the church. Upon his death, Dr. Santiago bequeathed this precious copy to the Pope, as a testimony of

gratitude for the many spiritual favors which the Supreme
Pontiff had granted to the Congregation of Our Lady, and as
a memento of his loyalty and esteem. When the Holy Father
received the image, he placed it in a golden frame and set it
next to his bed. Obliged by the disastrous events of 1848 to
leave the Papal States, His Holiness was barely able to gather
together a few personal effects. One of these was the sacred
image of Our Lady of the Angels.

It is a matter of record that Countess de Spaurs, wife of
the Bavarian minister, by her zeal and courage, contributed
greatly to the safety of the Supreme Pontiff, accompanying him
to Gaeta, the fortress where he found sanctuary. Upon his
return to the Papal States, the Pope considered he could make
no greater recompense to the lady who had rendered such outstanding service to his own person and to her holy religion,
than to present her with the image which had shared his trials
and his exile. This precious gift is treasured by the family of
the Countess, both for him who presented it, and even more
for her whom it represents.

On the twenty-second of November, 1852, Señor Martínez,
a young man of twenty-five years, attached to the Spanish
Legation in Rome, was mortally wounded by accident. His
youth, his personable character, his position, all contributed to
make the misfortune deeply felt. All of Rome took such a
great interest in his case that even people who did not know
him by sight prayed for his recovery. The corps of specialists
summoned to his bedside gave not the slightest hope for his
life. The Holy Father sent his personal blessing, and Cardinal
Antonelli, Secretary of State, personally visited the young man.

Countess de Spaurs, who knew the young man and thought
highly of him, went to his home, taking with her the image
of Our Lady of the Angels. The young man received the image
with great faith, embracing it and calling upon Our Lady not

to leave him for a moment. In spite of the opinion of his physicians, he began to recover immediately, so that everyone called the case a veritable resurrection. He himself attributed it entirely to Our Lady of the Angels. He had a copy of the image made, Pope Pius IX blessed it, and the young man took it to Spain to place it in the hands of his parents.

The visitor to the shrine of Our Lady of the Angels in Mexico City must be convinced that a special Providence watches over the image. Let us recapitulate its remarkable history.

In the great floods of 1604, 1607 and 1629 the barrio of Coatlán was virtually destroyed. The chapel of Isayoque lost its roof, doors, and walls, with only the principal wall, containing the image, left standing and exposed to the elements. From 1629 this wall, of the most inferior adobe, was covered with water *for five years,* up to the face and hands of the image. The features of the Virgin withstood more than four thousand rainstorms in that time. Mysteriously, the adobe was able to resist the corrosive effects of the saltpeter in which the soil abounds. Later, the image was covered with wet mats and boards nailed into its adobe wall for six months. This latter circumstance alone should have destroyed it completely. Yet it was found radiant with beauty, the hands and face showing not the slightest disfiguration. The conservation of the image in a combination of such unfavorable circumstances can only be called miraculous.

From the time when the *cacique* Isayoque erected the adobe wall and commissioned an unknown artist to paint the image in 1580, the face and hands have not been retouched in the slightest, nor has the wall been rebuilt! Surely Our Lady of the Angels must be guarding, from her heavenly throne, with a special predilection, her sacred image in Mexico.

X

NUESTRA SEÑORA DEL PUEBLITO

(OUR LADY OF EL PUEBLITO)

Villa La Corregidora, Querétaro

SIX miles north of the city of Querétaro, in Villa La Corregidora, is the church known as El Santuario. Here is
enshrined a three-centuries-old image of the Virgin Mary,
venerated far and wide under the name of Our Lady of El
Pueblito. It is the work of the sculptor monk Fray Sebastián
Gallegos, and was presented in the year 1635 to Padre Nicolás
de Zamora, pastor of the parish in what was then called El
Pueblito.

The venerable Padre de Zamora burned with zeal to convert the Chichimecas and the Otomies who inhabited the territory. But it seemed impossible to uproot their pagan practices
and to win them over to Christianity. In vain he preached the
word of God in their midst. It was as though they were listen-
ing to a strange language, watching the motion of his lips but
hearing only unintelligible sounds. Few, if any, were moved
to receive baptism, and even these, it appeared, reverted to
their idol-worship as soon as the man of God left their midst.

In the outskirts of Querétaro, especially on a hilltop near
the pueblo later known as San Francisco Galileo, the natives
had built places for worship of their idols. Here they gave
themselves up to their pagan cult. This brought grief to the

58

OUR LADY OF EL PUEBLITO
Villa La Corregidora, Querétaro

soul of Padre de Zamora, who could find no means to change the situation.

When the pastor received the image of the Virgin, he decided to place it in the open air, facing the hill upon which the cult of the idols was practiced. The effect was remarkable.

The natives came in groups to see the altar erected by Padre de Zamora. They gazed upon the delicate features of the sacred image. According to tradition, they burst spontaneously into songs of praise, a far cry from the furious combats and frenzied dances with which they honored their idols.

Now the preaching of the priest was received with welcome; it seemed scarcely necessary to enkindle their desire for Christianity or devotion to their new-found Faith. Padre de Zamora erected in the same place a little chapel, within which the statue reposed, and the Indians came in ever-increasing numbers.

From that time on the image came to be called "Our Lady of El Pueblito." In 1686 a confraternity was formed with the chief aim of building a suitable shrine for the advancement of the devotion to Our Lady. However, the poverty of the region was almost as great as the fervor of the people, and the project had to be postponed for lack of funds. For eighty-two years, during which Our Lady of El Pueblito was the center of devotion for the people of Querétaro and the surrounding countryside, the image remained in its small chapel. Then the religious were able to build a more capacious one, dedicated in 1714. Here the statue remained for some thirty-one years.

About this time one of the confraternity's benefactors, Capitán Don Pedro de Urtíaga, fell seriously ill. He made a vow to leave a part of his considerable revenues to erect a church, if given time to arrange his affairs. His prayer was granted and he recovered. Upon his death, the fulfillment of the promise was left to his son, Coronel Don José de Urtíaga. The latter carried the project through with zeal and efficiency. The funds left in Don Pedro's will erected a small shrine, and in 1745 Our Lady's image was translated there. This is the present-day shrine. Here, annually on the eighth of December, the Feast of the Immaculate Conception, the image is venerated with great solemnity. The devotion of the faithful has enriched it with many jewels and changes of vestment for the Virgin. These are housed, when not in use, in a handsome *camarín* added later in the rear of the sanctuary. After the erection of El Santuario, the Franciscan Fathers built there a guest house to facilitate and increase devotion to Our Lady of El Pueblito. In 1766 this hospice was made a regular Franciscan convent and house of recollection.

The sacred image of Our Lady of El Pueblito is carved of wood, the entire body in one piece. It measures about sixteen inches in height. The expression of the features is sweet, yet at the same time regal. In the words of an early chronicler, the Virgin's face "has the softness of the Maiden and the majesty of the Queen." The Divine Infant accompanies His Mother, but does not rest in her arms, like a child. Rather, like the Lord of Creation that He is, He stands at her right hand, on a small column. The figure of Saint Francis, on his knees, serves as pedestal for the Virgin. The Little Poor Man of Assisi bears on his hands the wounds of the Stigmata, and supports with his head and arms the three golden globes, or worlds, upon which Our Lady stands.

The devotion of the people of Querétaro to Our Lady of El Pueblito almost surpasses belief. Every year she is carried in procession to San Francisco, the Mother Church of Querétaro, for a solemn novena — nine days of prayer. On other occasions, especially in times of great public calamity, the same demonstration of faith in Our Lady's intercession takes

place. Many thousands of people always take part in the procession from El Pueblito to Querétaro, and scores of thousands
line the roads along the way, and the streets of Querétaro
leading to the church. Business along the line of march comes
to a standstill, and other traffic as well. On her annual pilgrimage to Querétaro, Our Lady visits all the Franciscan parishes in the city, remaining some days in each one. The devout
parishioners of each church vie with those of the others in
showing honor to their Sovereign Queen and Patroness.

We have already noted the wonders which Our Lady of
El Pueblito worked in drawing the pagan Indians from their
idolatrous practices into the sweet slavery of her service. In
addition there are innumerable well-authenticated cures and
favors attributed to her sovereign intercession. The one that
follows is related by Padre Francisco de Florencia, in his
monumental *Zodiaco Mariano.*

In the year 1733, according to the annual custom, the Holy
Virgin was brought in procession to Querétaro. At that time
Don Salvador Cervantes had been crippled for many months.
As he lived in a house not very far from the church where the
Virgin would stop, Don Salvador decided that his sons should
dress him and take him to the church to pray to the Virgin
for his cure. But the sons would not agree to do this, because
of the painful condition of the sick man. Instead they carried
him to a low balcony overlooking the street, whence he might
be able to see the pastor take the image from the coach in
which it was borne.

The balcony was about sixty yards from the point where
the coach stopped. As a religious went up to the coach to
receive the Virgin from the hands of the *cura,* the mules
drawing the coach suddenly bolted with it. They did not stop
until the coach was opposite the balcony of Don Salvador.
There the pastor dismounted with the sacred image, and the

sick man had the good fortune to be able to touch it. With great confidence he begged of the Holy Virgin the grace of being restored to health. At that moment he recovered, and descended from the balcony, walking for the first time in many months, and as healthy as if he had never been crippled. This remarkable incident was witnessed by crowds of people.

In the canonical process of authenticating the wonders attributed to the intercession of Our Lady of El Pueblito is a mass of sworn testimony which has been collected relative to the sacred image. Many witnesses have testified to seeing a shining star above the forehead of the image, as if to signal that Mary is the Guide and North Star for the people of Querétaro.

Nor should we think it strange that such prodigies occur even in our day of science and skepticism. For a mother loves all her children, though some be grown to man's estate and others be still small. The way she speaks to the child will be different from the way she addresses his older brother and sister, for what appeals to one may be beyond the comprehension of the other. And it must delight the heart of the Mother of mankind to visit those of her children who receive her with such childlike faith. From them, surely, the kingdom of heaven is never far away.

OUR LADY HEALTH OF THE SICK

Pátzcuaro, Michoacán

XI

NUESTRA SEÑORA DE LA SALUD

(OUR LADY HEALTH OF THE SICK)

Pátzcuaro, Michoacán

$\mathcal{A}$ S THE Chevalier Beaumont noted in his diary, Pátzcuaro was formerly known as "the place of tears and mourning" because the Tarascans went thither to weep for their people slain in wars or in sacrifice to the gods. Long before Columbus set foot upon the shores of the New World, the Tarascan annals spoke of Pátzcuaro as the city where arose the altars of their gods, where the chiefs of their priestly caste lived, and where kings and their court came to play. But, continues Beaumont, when the teachings of Christianity took root in the hearts of the Tarascans, "Pátzcuaro" in their language came to mean "place of joy and delights."

The chief credit for the Christianization of the Tarascans must go to one of New Spain's outstanding statesmen, who became one of her greatest churchmen. Under the infamous Nuño de Guzmán, president of the ill-starred First Audiencia, the Spanish Conquest in Mexico had begun to degenerate into sheer exploitation of the Indians, with cruelty and rapine the order of the day. The great cities of Michoacán, including Pátzcuaro and Tzintzuntzán, dwelling places of kings, were emptied, and whole communities fled into the mountain fastnesses. In consequence the work of the first missionaries in

Michoacán was completely destroyed. At this point, in 1533, the Spanish Crown sent a Second Audiencia, a group of men with power in Mexico subordinate only to that of the king himself. Distinguished even among these outstanding men by his special qualities was Don Vasco de Quiroga. Working efficiently and wisely, Quiroga carried out his monarch's will; the abuses of Guzmán were remedied, the deserted cities of Michoacán repopulated, the missionary *frailes* brought back. At the request of Charles V, the Holy See in 1537 named Vasco de Quiroga, then sixty-eight years old, bishop of the newly erected Diocese of Michoacán.

In Pátzcuaro, on the shores of the lake which bears its name, Bishop Quiroga met his greatest challenge. The Tarascan priestly caste was intrenched there, and the priests, walled behind strong fortifications, and defying Crown and Church, continued their pagan rituals. But even their understandable hatred of the Spaniard and consequent distrust for the Spaniards' God were not proof against the indefatigable charity of "Tata Vasco" (Father Vasco), as the Indians soon came to call their bishop. Something more than a year after his consecration, he had persuaded one of the Tarascan priests, an expert sculptor of idols, to fashion for the Christian community an image of the Virgin Mary! It is that same image which we know and venerate today as *Nuestra Señora de la Salud* — "Our Lady Health of the Sick." The reason for the name given is bound up with the apostolic labors of Vasco de Quiroga.

While Don Vasco was still with the Audiencia as a civil servant of the Crown, he had founded, among other charitable works, a hospital for Indians in the pueblo of Santa Fe in Mexico, a few kilometers from the center of the capital. As bishop, he built another in Pátzcuaro, dedicated to Saint Martha. Within the hospital chapel he placed the image of

Our Lady, under whose protection the bishop consecrated his Tarascans. Our Lady accepted the charge. Soon tales of remarkable favors and cures granted at her feet began to spread throughout the region. And, whereas before only the poorest Indians had come to pray in the little hospital chapel, soon the Indian leaders and the haughty Spanish *encomenderos* and their families also flocked into the sanctuary, drawn by their own needs and the reports of Our Lady's generosity. Before long, both Indian and Spaniard referred to the image in the Hospital of Saint Martha as *"La Salud de Los Enfermos"* — Health of the Sick. When Bishop de Quiroga died in 1565, at the age of ninety-six, universally loved by his people, the fame of his *Virgen de la Salud* was known throughout Mexico.

An important phase in the later history of *Nuestra Señora* begins toward the end of the seventeenth century, when Dr. Juan Meléndez Carreño was named pastor of Pátzcuaro. Known and respected both for his virtues and his achievements in the field of letters, Father Meléndez owed his life to a remarkable cure granted by Our Lady of Pátzcuaro. When he was appointed to the parish in 1690, the priest made it his care to promote continued devotion to Our Lady. One colorful means employed was a weekly procession. Every Saturday Our Lady would be taken through the streets of Pátzcuaro, accompanied by the clergy and outstanding citizens of the town, with lights and music, and the chanting of the fifteen Mysteries of the Rosary. Much of the legend and tradition concerning the statue centers around the period of Father Meléndez.

It will be remembered that in the seventeenth century there came into popular vogue the custom of vesting images of the Virgin with costly fabrics and jewels. From its origins in Spain, the practice spread to the colonies. Padre Meléndez, to show his devotion and to foster Our Lady's cult, wished to apparel

her statue in such a manner. The design of the image rendering this impractical, he conceived the idea of removing the
lower portion of the figure, which was made of light reed
cane, and retaining little more than the head and arms.

Although Bishop de Ortega Montanés had given Padre
Meléndez permission to make the requested modifications in
the image, the project did not meet with the approval of the
Indians, nor, to be fair, of a goodly number of the Spanish
community. The Indians, for their part, were used to their
Virgin Mother — their *Naná Yurixe,* as they called her in the
Tarascan tongue — and did not want her to be changed. And
a party of the Spaniards, led by the *Licendiado* Juan de Pedraza,
said they would spend their last *duro* and leave no stone un-
turned to prevent the padre from cutting the image to bits.
For, they asked with considerable logic, had not the image
been designed in that fashion by their beloved Bishop Quiroga,
and blessed by his own venerable hands? And there was a
great deal to be said for this viewpoint.

Nevertheless (so runs the oft-repeated local legend),
Padre Meléndez determined to go ahead with his plan. One
night, he had the image taken from its niche and brought in
secret to the sacristy, where several sculptors, under the super-
vision of the clergy, would make the required modifications.
But lo! when the artisans picked up hammer and chisel to
begin, the face of the Virgin assumed an expression of great
affliction, and sweat began to pour copiously from its features.
The workmen were terror-stricken, and could not continue.
Father Meléndez was considerably disturbed by this turn of
events, and although his heart was set on embellishing the
statue, he decided to forego the project. At this point, his
assistant, Don Cristobal de Molina, made a suggestion: Why
not consult the Jesuit Father Bernard Rolandegui, Rector of

the College at Pátzcuaro and a distinguished theologian? Perhaps he would be able to advise them. Father Rolandegui heard the account, and recommended that the clergy pray to Our Lady before the image, begging her permission to make her likeness more beautiful. After this was done, the afflicted expression disappeared from the features of the image, and the project went forward. On one point, however, Our Lady remained firm: the head and hands were not to be retouched. When the artisans attempted to repair one of the eyebrows, which had been scarred, the varnish would not remain on the spot, but kept dropping off. To this day the slight imperfection can be noted. After the *corpus* of the figure had been planed and chiseled down, it was covered with Breton lawn and then gilded. At this point an ancient inscription, half erased by time, came to light. *"Salus Infirmorum,"* it read — Health of the Sick.

During the days when the modifications to the statue were being made, necessarily in secret, there were some anxious moments. It will be recalled that Don Juan de Pedraza, in particular, was determined not to allow any retouching of the image. One night, suspecting that there was something afoot, he went to the hospital, where a Lay Brother, Francisco Yañez, acted as sacristan.

"I promise you, Francisco," Pedraza had threatened him, "if I ever come here and find you have let the image out of this chapel, your life will not be worth a *centavito!"*

Fearing something of the kind, Father Meléndez had placed in the niche another image of the Virgin, praying that it would pass for the original when viewed at a distance and through partly drawn curtains.

When the *Licendiado* arrived at the hospital, he was the soul of charm.

"Ah, *mi amigo,* Don Francisco!" he greeted the sacristan, giving him a hearty *abrazo.* "How goes it with you?"

But Francisco Yañez was not deceived by the other's cordiality, and trembled to think what might happen if the *Licenciado* should take it into his head to visit the chapel. And that is exactly what Pedraza had in mind.

"Come, my friend," he said, "let us go to the chapel. I am anxious to pray before the Virgin for a few moments."

The frightened sacristan had no choice, and soon they stood before the altar in the gloom of the chapel.

"Light some candles, if you will," said Don Juan de Pedraza; then: "More candles, so I can see Our Lady better"; the next moment: "Open the curtains, man! Be quick about it!"

In fear and trembling the sacristan did as he was told. Pedraza mounted the altar steps and peered at the image, scrutinizing it carefully. Then, to the amazement of Francisco, who had been watching for signs of rage over the substitution, the face of the *Licenciado* broke out into a beatific smile.

"Beautiful, beautiful!" he murmured. "We cannot let anyone alter this beautiful image of the Virgin, can we, Francisco?"

"N-no, Señor," stammered the amazed sacristan.

"And remember, *amigo,*" called back the *Licenciado* as he mounted horse and prepared to ride off, "I shall hold you personally responsible!"

When Father Meléndez and the other priests heard the story next day from the lips of Francisco, they were devoutly impressed, feeling that Our Lady herself must have intervened to satisfy the *Licenciado.* For of course there was very little resemblance between the two statues.

After the image had been refinished and dressed in the flowing garments very much like those she wears today, *Nuestra Señora de la Salud* was returned to her chapel. Of course, when the people, Tarascans and Spaniards alike, saw Our Lady in her new regalia, they were delighted, and even Juan de Pedraza and his party had to admit that the appearance had been much improved. There was another problem, though. In her new garments, Our Lady made the old chapel under its roof of *barro* seem shabbier than ever, and so Padre Meléndez determined to build a new sanctuary. The funds, collected throughout Michoacán and later throughout all of Mexico between 1691 and 1717, resulted in the construction of a fine temple, dedicated in 1717 on December 8, feast of the Immaculate Conception. Later (1893), a new altar was dedicated on the same feast. Solemn coronation of the image of *Nuestra Señora de la Salud* was decreed in a Pontifical Brief of His Holiness Leo XIII dated April 5, 1898. The actual coronation was accomplished on the feast of the Immaculate Conception in 1899 by the Archbishop of Michoacán, Don José Ignacio Arciga: this was almost the last official act of the venerable prelate.

Nuestra Señora de la Salud remained in her temple until 1908. On June 29, 1907, the parish church had been erected by St. Pius X into a collegiate church with its chapter of canons, and the same year a new altar was built. It had originally been designed to be the cathedral of Michoacán, and its construction as such sanctioned in 1550 by Pope Julian III; but the plans were not carried through, since the episcopal See was moved to Valladolid (now Morelia). On January 8, 1908, the Virgin's image was removed to its present location above the principal altar.

The Jesuit Father Pedro Sarmiento has compiled a list of *milagros,* or extraordinary favors, attributed to the intercession

of Our Lady of Pátzcuaro, Health of the Sick. All of these
have been attested to by people worthy of credence, either personal beneficiaries or qualified eyewitnesses.

During Pátzcuaro's great epidemic of 1692, in which many
met their death, the pastor, Padre Meléndez, determined to
dedicate nine days of prayer to the Virgin, taking her image
in procession through the streets of the city and into all
the barrios. The morning after the procession, when Father
Meléndez entered the church to offer the first of the nine days'
Masses, he saw that the image had a star upon the forehead.
Calling Don Francisco Lerín, a devout Spaniard who, in spite
of his great wealth, dedicated himself to the care of Our Lady's
sanctuary, the priest asked:

"Who has put that star on the Virgin's forehead?"

"Not I, padre," replied Don Francisco, turning to look at
the image. To be sure, a bright star shone on the brow of the
statue, clearly visible to all who had crowded into the church
to attend Mass. From that moment the epidemic began to
abate noticeably, the deaths stopped, the sick experienced im-
provement. And, as the plague diminished, so did the brightness of the star. Finally, on the last day of the novena, when
the plague had vanished, the mysterious star was no longer
to be seen. Since then, at various times in the history of Our
Lady Health of the Sick, trustworthy witnesses have reported
seeing the same phenomenon, and each time it has been the
prelude to some notable event in the history of the image or
to the granting of some remarkable favor.

Among the records of the sanctuary is the sworn deposition made by a Spanish General, Don Manuel de las Heras.
His wife, Doña Gerónima, confined to her bed with a raging
fever, had for days grown steadily weaker. Ultimately the
physicians despaired of her life.

"I must not die now," she said to her husband. "Bring me the image of Our Lady from the *templo*." Permission was granted to take the statue to his house, and Don Manuel, accompanied by a great company of friends and neighbors, carried it through the streets to the sick woman's side. Doña Gerónima slept quietly through that night, and awakening the next morning, found herself strong and well.

An equally well-verified event of a different nature concerns the drought of 1692. Although the middle of June had arrived, and the rains were long months overdue, the skies remained unclouded. The crops on the haciendas were burning up, there was no pasture for the cattle and sheep, and Lake Pátzcuaro had fallen to so low a level that most of the fish died, and the fishermen who made their living on the water were unable to work. The workers petitioned the pastor for permission to carry the Virgin's image through the streets. At noon the procession prepared to leave the church, under a blue and cloudless sky, with *Nuestra Señora de la Salud*. The *anda,* or platform upon which the image was to be transported, stood ready in the sanctuary, supported upon the stout shoulders of four men, and a number of priests, who were to accompany the procession, stood at the altar to receive Our Lady as she was taken from her shrine. As the cloth covering was removed and the officials began to take the image from the niche, the sky suddenly darkened and rain began to fall gently. There was no thunder, no lightning; the rain increased in intensity and continued in abundance until three o'clock. The drought had been broken, and from then on throughout the wet season, every day brought its normal quota of rain. The intercession of *Nuestra Señora de la Salud* was acknowledged by all. On other occasions since that time the Virgin has been invoked successfully to bring rain for her devotees in Pátzcuaro.

There are several memorable instances on record of Our
Lady of Pátzcuaro being invoked to renew the well or spring
upon which a community depended. The following example
is typical: In 1714, in the villa of Pinzándaro, there was a large
ranch whose spring, at which all the cattle were watered, had
dried up early in the year. In the middle of June that year,
a pilgrim image of Our Lady of Pátzcuaro passed through the
villa, on a mission of alms-raising for the yet-to-be-completed
sanctuary. Don Fernando Vaca, Colonel in the armies of the
Crown and Lieutenant-general of Pinzándaro, went to the pastor, Don Salvador Servino, who was *comisario* of the Holy
Office in the district.

"Padre," he requested, "let us take *la Virgen* in procession
to the Rancho Huitzo, and have Holy Mass there. Perhaps,
through the intercession of *Nuestra Señora,* the spring will
flow again."

On June 15, the image was taken in procession to the ranch.
While the altar was being arranged for Mass, one Juan Manuel
Cantor tested the dry spring bed to a palm's depth and found
only dried earth. When the Mass had been offered, water
began to spurt up from the well, soon filling it. In addition,
more than a dozen other springs appeared around the original
one, so that, where there had been a shallow hole before, now
there was a good-sized arroyo. This occurrence was deposed
and sworn to by the officials mentioned and by many other
qualified witnesses.

These are only a few of many cases on record testify-
ing to the devotion of the people of Pátzcuaro — and of all
Michoacán, for that matter — to their Virgin, Our Lady Health
of the Sick. But besides these remarkable instances which history has recorded, there is the living, present-day devotion of
the *patzcuarenses* to the Virgin and her image. You will see it
all about you in the region: in the little household shrines that

display her image, and in the shops as well, and on the faces of the people as they enter *La Colegiata* to see *La Virgencita,* or leave the church after morning Mass or evening devotions. And surely "Tata Vasco," whose name is still on the lips of his beloved Indians at Pátzcuaro after four centuries, must be more satisfied with their devotion to the Virgin than with any other evidence of his labors in Michoacán.

XII

NUESTRA SEÑORA DE LA LUZ

(OUR LADY OF THE LIGHT)

Salvatierra, Guanajuato

*c*A SACRED image of Our Lady, which today reposes in "the ancient, noble, and most loyal city of San Andrés de Salvatierra," is known and venerated under the title *Nuestra Señora de la Luz,* that is, "Our Lady of Light." In the early seventeenth century, this image occupied a small chapel in the Indian pueblo of Guatzindeo, in a valley of the same name, across the Rio Lerma from Salvatierra. This pueblo was part of the Hacienda San Buenaventura, whose proprietor was a certain Don Antonio Martín Tamayo. How the sacred image became known as "Our Lady of the Light" is a favorite legend among the townsfolk.

On various nights, Don Antonio, along with a Franciscan religious, had observed lights blazing from one of the rooms in a hospice of the pueblo, so as to make it appear as if the room were on fire. Don Antonio sent servants to ascertain the cause of the light. The servants returned, to say that there was no fire nor light in the room. Don Antonio and the religious then went personally to the hospice. In the mysterious room they found a number of old and discarded objects, among them an image of Our Lady, considerably damaged. Don Antonio took the statue to his hacienda, and afterward sent it

74

OUR LADY OF THE LIGHT

Salvatierra, Guanajuato

to Pátzcuaro to be repaired. Struck by the surpassing beauty of the renovated image, the pious Spaniard built a chapel to house it. Therein the Tamayo family placed the image for public veneration. Because of the events already described, they named it Our Lady of the Light, although the title remained merely a popular, unofficial one for some years.

According to common tradition dating back three and a half centuries, the image was seen, during many nights and by many people, to put forth great lights and reflections, both in its own chapel and later in the churches of Salvatierra during the course of pilgrimages. Soon repeated favors and marvels attributed to Our Lady of the Light were known far and wide. Devotees flocked to the chapel, not merely from the city of Salvatierra and its environs, but even from far away places, to find consolation and help in their problems.

Each year, during the season of the rains, the citizens of Salvatierra would bear "Our Lady of the Valley," as they also called her, in procession from the little chapel in Guatzindeo across the Rio Lerma to the city. Amid great demonstrations of faith and confidence in Our Lady's intercession, they would pray for the rainfall necessary to a plentiful harvest. At other times, during plagues and other public calamities, they would do likewise. It is related that prompt answer to their prayers was always forthcoming.

On one occasion, the Bishop of Valladolid, Don Juan de Ortega Montañes, on a journey to Mexico City, fell seriously ill while passing through Salvatierra. Our Lady's image at that time was being venerated in the Church of Our Lady of Carmen. Having great devotion to the Virgin, Bishop Ortega offered Mass at her altar. Immediately afterward he experienced a return of health, and was able to continue the journey. The prelate attributed this remarkable blessing to Our Lady, and officially bestowed upon her the title, *Nuestra*

Señora de la Luz. From that time to the present she has been called "Our Lady of the Light."

A document of the year 1676 relates, among other sworn testimony, the following incident:

"Many are the wonders which this sacred image has worked. For instance, when it began to be venerated in its first chapel, the undersigned witness knows that one night a thief entered to rob her of her crown and jewels. The thief confessed later that when he tried to take the crown, the sacred image turned away her sovereign countenance, without letting him despoil her of her crown. [For this reason today the image has the head inclined to one side, it is said.] And that neither was he able to leave the chapel, until, on the following day, the story was told to one of the Alcaldes Ordinary, a certain Aguirre. This latter had him strangled to death, and his body set, as an example and warning, at the entrance of the bridge.

"Other wonders are so common and so frequent through the favor of Her Majesty, for the succor, patronage, and benefit of this city, that everyone can testify to them, as is evident. For all know that when they need rain, as soon as they take their case to the Lady for prosecution, she obtains rain for them. The same thing happens when any disease, plague, or epidemic begins. Relief comes quickly, as soon as it is asked for."

On one occasion, Our Lady was brought to Salvatierra for nine days of prayer in connection with some public necessity. As the bearers were carrying the statue on its platform through the low doors of the entrance, the head was struck against the top of the door, badly disfiguring the face. The disconsolate parishioners were at their wits' end, considering the image beyond repair. Suddenly a man in the rough clothes of an artisan made his appearance. Asserting that he was by trade a sculptor, he offered to repair the statue, without setting a definite price for his services. The parishioners at first met the offer with understandable reservations, but the problem admitted of no delay. The novena had begun, crowds were coming from far and near, and the image could not be exposed for veneration in its damaged state without causing scandal. So they agreed to let him undertake the assignment.

Early next morning the artisan arrived and set to work. They offered him some chocolate, which he refused. Later they brought him a meal, which he likewise refused. In the early afternoon he came out, saying that the repairs were completed and the image needed but a few hours in the sun to dry. Once again he refused food, and left. All that afternoon the officials waited for him to return and present his bill, but in vain. Inquiries were made, but the anonymous workman had disappeared without a trace. To this day he remains unknown. Certain it is, however, that he was an artisan of great talent and skill, for the image of Our Lady of the Light shows no trace of the accident.

In the year 1743, the *Ayuntamiento* (municipal government) of Salvatierra petitioned the Crown for the privilege of building a sanctuary for *La Virgen de la Luz*. The Viceroy, Conde de Fuenclara, approved the venture, and construction began in that year. From 1808 to the present day, the blessed image has been venerated in that sanctuary.

His Holiness Pope Pius XI granted the honors of Pontifical Coronation to the image of *Nuestra Señora de la Luz* in a Papal Brief dated the sixteenth of September, 1938. The Archbishop of Morelia, Dr. Don Leopoldo Ruiz y Flores, crowned the venerable statue with a golden diadem, in the name of the Supreme Pontiff, on May 24, 1939.

XIII

NUESTRA SEÑORA DE LOS MILAGROS DE TLALTENANGO

(OUR LADY OF MIRACLES)

Tlaltenango, Morelos

O N THE outskirts of Cuernavaca to the north, on the main road to Mexico City, lies the ancient pueblo of Tlalte-nango. Perhaps we should more properly say it "clings" to the hills through which the road dips, climbs and twists. The very name *Tlaltenango,* in Nahuatl, the tongue of the Aztecs, signifies "Place of the Wall of Earth." Hernán Cortés entered here in 1521, and erected a church in honor of San José in 1523. Thus the original church antedates by two years the Church of San Francisco in Mexico City, which Motolinía called the first church to be erected in the Indies!

Here also, in 1535, the Conquistador built the first sugar mill in the Americas, remnants of which can still be seen. Soon the chapel erected by Cortés was too small to accommodate the sugar workers and their families, so another church was built, wall to wall with the original. The second church, named in honor of Saint Jerome, was erected in the second half of the sixteenth century. In this latter church today is the shrine of Our Lady of Tlaltenango. Tourists on their way to Cuernavaca, Taxco, or Acapulco may catch a glimpse of the church minutes after leaving the toll road from Mexico, and the devout will want to pay a visit to the shrine.

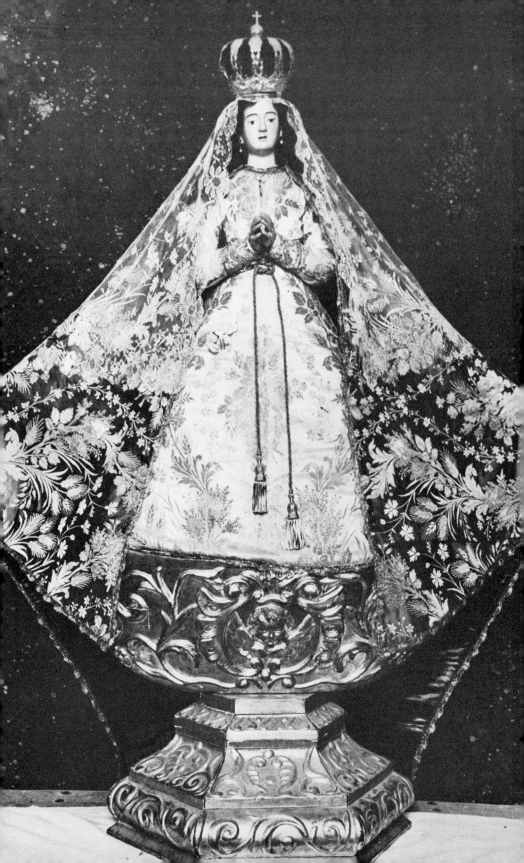

OUR LADY OF MIRACLES
Tlaltenango, Morelos

The tradition of this venerated image can be traced back to 1720. According to legend, toward the end of May in that year, two young men were journeying along the road from Acapulco, where they had presumably arrived by ship. They stopped for rest and lodging at the *posada* (small hostelry) of Doña Agustina Andrade, in Tlaltenango. Genteel and handsome, they created something of a sensation in that pueblo. The travelers remained overnight, and upon leaving they entrusted to their hostess' care a richly decorated casket, to be guarded until their return. Days and weeks went by, but the *caballeros* did not come back to claim their property.

One night, some two months later, the good lady heard music through the doors of the room where she kept the treasure. She roused her family, and they entered the room. Along with the strains of celestial music, they became aware of rays of light emanating from the casket, together with an exotic perfume. All agreed to preserve secrecy concerning the marvelous happening, for fear that the authorities would confiscate the mysterious box, which by now they considered their own. But good intentions could not withstand their desire to share with the townsfolk their enchanting discovery, and soon the facts were public property. There was no recourse but to notify the ecclesiastical and civil authorities.

On August the thirtieth, Doña Agustina went to Cuernavaca on that mission. She related the happenings first to Fray Pedro de Arana, pastor of the Church of the Assumption (now the cathedral) and Guardian of the Franciscan Convent. Then she visited the *Alcalde Mayor* at the Palacio, who promised to make a joint inspection with Fray Pedro that same evening.

Making the journey on foot with their attendants, so as not to attract attention, the representatives of Church and Crown arrived at the *posada* in Tlaltenango. Ordering the lights to be extinguished, they entered the room where the mysterious box lay. As their eyes became accustomed to the darkness, the casket was seen to throw out soft rays of light. To their nostrils came the delightful fragrance of an exotic perfume. When Fray Pedro pried loose the box cover, the astonished onlookers beheld a statue of the Virgin, richly vested in rose tunic and blue cloak. They bore it in procession to the old Church of San José. The next day a novena was begun with a Solemn Mass, ending on the eighth of September, the Feast of the Nativity of the Blessed Virgin. So runs the legend. Since 1720 the tradition has been commemorated each year with a *fiesta* on that date.

The innumerable favors granted to the devotees of the sacred image have earned for it the title *Nuestra Señora de los Milagros* (Our Lady of Miracles). She is especially invoked by expectant mothers for the grace of a safe delivery in childbirth. The many ex-votos of gold and silver, marble and wood, which decorate the sanctuary, bear eloquent witness to the gratitude of those whom Our Lady has favored.

On the eighth of December, 1954, the Most Reverend Sergio Méndez Arceo, seventh Bishop of Cuernavaca, placed upon the forehead of Our Lady of Miracles a golden crown. The coronation symbolizes the rule of Mary as Queen and official Patroness of the City and Diocese of Cuernavaca.

OUR LADY OF THE OAK
Monterrey, Nuevo León

XIV

NUESTRA SEÑORA DEL ROBLE

(OUR LADY OF THE OAK)

Monterrey, Nuevo León

𝒯HE American in Mexico traveling by road to or from the eastern United States border, will ordinarily pass through Monterrey. Set in the valley of the Rio Santa Catarina and ringed about by mountains, this "Chicago of Mexico" is the most prosperous, and at the same time, one of the most attractive cities in the republic.

Its present appearance and status are a far cry from what they were in the time of the Conquistadors. In 1560, when Francisco de Urdiñola entered the region he called Nuevo León, he found the valley inhabited by nomadic bands of Indians who lived by hunting. In 1579 there was a little pueblo known as Santa Lucía, with a handful of Spaniards and some natives. In 1585 Santa Lucía became La Ciudad de Léon.

To the four Spanish families and the scattering of natives who colonized the first settlement, it must have seemed a veritable paradise. The founder, Don Pedro Rodriguez, called it " . . . a peaceful and healthful place with a temperate climate, good air and water, and many fruit trees. It has many mountains and ponds, springs, and land to till, and many silver mines."

In such a setting did Our Lady deign to show herself in a special manner to a young shepherdess. The legend has all the charm and freshness of a tale from the *Fioretti* of Saint Francis.

When the early Franciscans were journeying to the northern part of New Spain to spread the Gospel of Christ, they came to the valley of the Rio Santa Catarina. In the hollow of a large and spreading oak tree, they found a natural shrine for an image of the Virgin, which they placed therein. While they remained in the vicinity, the little shrine served for their devotions to the Mother of God. How long the missionaries remained we do not know. Perhaps they waited to preach the word of God to roving tribes who never appeared. At all events, the day came when they had to move on. And Our Lady's image remained behind, in its leafy hermitage. Why did the saintly missionaries leave the image of their Sovereign there? Was their departure so precipitate that they had no time to return to the chapel in the oak? The answers must remain shrouded in the mists of the past. Perhaps — and this seems most likely — the good *frailes,* who certainly had placed the land and their mission under Mary's patronage, left her image to watch over this chosen part of her domain.

The years went by and the little community of Ciudad León flourished. On the twentieth of September, 1596, the ninth Viceroy of New Spain, Don Gaspar de Zuñiga y Acevedo, Conde de Monterrey, named it *La Ciudad Metropolitana de Nuestra Señora de Monterrey* ("The Metropolitan City of Our Lady of Monterrey"). And in the pastoral land outside the city, shepherds tended their flocks and husbandmen tilled the fields, while an oak tree guarded its treasure.

From her hiding place in the heart of the old tree, Our Lady looked upon these simple people and loved them. Each morning she saw them leave the grass-roofed *jacal* or adobe *casita,* ax or spade on shoulder, to wrest a living for their families from the good earth, or, with staff in hand, to drive sheep, goats, or cattle to pasture. Evenings, she saw them return, weary and sweat-soaked from toil, but smiling, to their homes. Our Lady watched the women and small children come out to receive their menfolk, and she saw the white smoke of a hundred chimneys signal the evening meal as the sun went down behind the mountains. And Mary smiled, too, and blessed them.

It was to a little shepherdess that *La Virgencita* revealed herself, mindful perhaps of a special kinship with the Divine Son who said, "I am the Good Shepherd." Who was the girl? The legend does not tell. She may have been descended from one of the early Spanish colonists, or from the natives who were among the first to receive the Faith in that region. With her little flock and a faithful dog, the child would take her sheep each morning and drive them to the grassy slopes near her home. In the cooler hours of the morning and later afternoon, they would graze at will, and during the heat of the day would rest in shade, under the vigilant eye of the sheep dog, while their young mistress sought the shadowed coolness of a tree.

On one such day, the direction of the flock had taken them to a quiet bit of hilly pasture land. While the sun rode high in the heavens, the shepherdess took her simple meal beneath the boughs of a giant oak, the faithful dog at her feet. It was one of her favorite places, quiet, cool, and secluded, and she came to it often to enjoy the solitude. The hours passed pleasantly, and soon it was time to begin their leisurely homeward journey. Staff in hand, the girl prepared to round up her flock, when her attention was drawn by an opening in the tree trunk, just above her head. Her eyes momentarily blinded by the westerly sun, the cool darkness

in the shadow of the tree partially obscured her vision. And
then, as a shaft of light slanted down, she saw it — a motion-
less figure, standing within a niche of the trunk. She drew
closer. Yes, it was true. Her upraised glance beheld the
ancient image of the Virgin, just as the Franciscans had left
it, generations before.

With hurrying steps the little shepherdess guided her flock
down the rocky slope, across the meadows in the waning light
of that Mexican afternoon. Her words tumbling over one
another in their eagerness to be told, she poured forth to her
parents the tale of the Lady in the oak. Parents told neighbors,
and neighbors told one another, as the story raced through the
little community, and the good people flocked to the hillside.
There, in the shadow of the oak, they saw that it was as the
maiden had said. The venerable image, as regal and as sweet
as the Virgin to whom their daily prayer was directed, gazed
down upon them. With a holy gladness in their hearts, the
simple people took down the precious discovery and bore it
to the little chapel where they were accustomed to worship.
The news spread into the city, and the townsfolk came crowd-
ing into the sanctuary to see the marvel.

But, as the legend goes on to relate, Our Lady of the Oak
did not wish to remain in that place. After generations of star-
filled nights on the hillside, the darkness of the little shrine
did not please her. She returned one night to her tree-trunk
home, seeking to show in this way that she wished her temple
to be erected on that spot. The next morning she was found
again in the heart of the oak. Her mantle was covered with
brambles and dust, for she had made the journey walking, to
sanctify by her footsteps the land that she loved. Thus runs
the legend.

They built her a shrine upon the spot, and when time had
destroyed it, another made of stone. The third sanctuary, which

still holds the sacred image, dates from 1855. It is among the most beautiful of the churches in Monterrey. On the night of the twenty-fourth of October, 1905, its roof caved in, burying the sanctuary and the image under a pile of rubble. By the gracious intervention of Divine Providence, Our Lady's statue, found beneath tons of rock, remained unharmed.

Scarcely twenty inches in height, the image of Our Lady of the Oak is formed of a kind of clay made with cornstalks and called *pasta de Michoacán*. Her tunic and mantle are of brocade, richly embroidered. The noble ladies of Monterrey despoiled their jewel cases to enrich the crown of gold that adorns her brow.

Our Lady of the Oak has been made the official Patroness and Protectress of Monterrey. On the eighth of December each year, the Feast of the Immaculate Conception, Monterrey becomes a city of *fiesta* as the faithful gather from far and near to do homage to their Sovereign. Her church has been erected by the Holy Father into a basilica, and affiliated with the Roman Basilica of Saint John Lateran, the "Mistress and Mother" of the churches of Christendom.

XV

NUESTRA SEÑORA DE ZAPOPAN

(OUR LADY OF ZAPOPAN)

Zapopan, Jalisco

TODAY the village of Zapopan is a quiet little place not many miles from Guadalajara by an excellent highway. Its tranquillity and religious atmosphere must be a far cry from pre-Conquest times, when it was a feudal district and tributary of the powerful King of Tonalá. In those days the Indians of the district worshiped an idol called *Teopintzintl,* "The Child God," to which they offered gifts of hare and partridge. When the kingdom of Tonalá bowed to Nuño de Guzmán in 1530, Zapopan came under Spanish domain. The Indian queen, Chihuapili Tzapotzinco, ordered all the chieftains under her rule to render their obedience to the Spanish Crown, and in March of 1530 the cacique of Atemajac, under whose jurisdiction lay Zapopan, complied with this order. The Mixton War of 1541, however, depopulated the district, and the *encomendero* of Tlaltenango, Francisco de Bobadilla, obtained the Viceroy's permission to repopulate Zapopan with Indians from Tlaltenango, thus lessening the chance of another uprising.

On the eighth of December, 1541, the pueblo of Zapopan was resettled in accordance with the agreement, and on that day the Franciscan Fray Antonio de Segovia gave to the newly

86

OUR LADY OF ZAPOPAN
Zapopan, Jalisco

settled colony a small image of Our Lady of the Immaculate
Conception. For ten years it had accompanied him on his
apostolic journeys. In fact, only a short while before, while
the Mixton War was still in progress, Fray Antonio, with his
missionary companion Fray Miguel de Bolonia, had gone
among the warring Indians, the image about his neck, exhorting them to make peace with the Spaniards. It is related that
while Fray Antonio was preaching, the Indians saw luminous
rays issuing from the image of Our Lady, and that this fact,
as much as his preaching, caused them to stop fighting. In
thirty-six hours Fray Antonio de Segovia brought to the Viceroy for pardon more than six thousand Indians, who had laid
down their arms. From that time Fray Antonio called the
image *La Pacificadora* ("She Who Makes Peace").

The image is made of *pasta de Michoacán* — pieces of
cornstalk smoothed and cemented together by glue. It is little
more than thirteen inches in height, and represents the Virgin
Mary under her title of the Immaculate Conception. The
hands, joined before the breast, are of wood. The original
sculpture donated by Fray Antonio de Segovia consisted only
of the upper half, it is believed, the lower section having been
added at a later date. As the lower half is not in proportion
to the upper, the reconstruction gives a stunted effect to the
image. However, since the original sculptured garments nowa-
days are always covered with rich vestments of fabric, the
disproportion is not apparent.

In its sculptured form, the statue represents Our Lady
standing with her feet upon a rudely formed crescent moon.
She wears a red tunic and a dark blue mantle outlined in gold.
The eyes are painted, and the somewhat thick lips are closed.
One may find much to be desired in the image, considered as
a work of art. Yet we must remember that it has the honor
of being the first image of the Virgin Mary venerated in the

State of Jalisco, and that it has seen the Church in that part
of Mexico grow from the tiniest seed to the great, many-
branched tree of the present-day Catholic Faith. Furthermore,
for over four centuries, Our Lady of Zapopan has been a constant channel of heavenly favors to the people of Jalisco.

The image has many changes of vestment for various
occasions, all richly silvered and gilt, and enhanced by pearls
and precious stones. There are a gold-tasseled blue sash, in-
dicating military rank, and the gold baston of command corresponding to that rank, in the right hand; both usually worn
with each change of vestment. Our Lady also holds a golden
scepter and carries golden keys to the city.

On her head rests a jewel-encrusted golden crown, witnessing her Pontifical Coronation. The whole is surrounded
by an aureole of gold studded with jewels, and there is a
golden half-moon beneath the feet. A beautifully worked
pedestal of chased silver, ornamented with sculptured scenes
representing the statue's history, weighs over a hundred and
twenty pounds.

It was Diego de Herrera, pastor of Zapopan from 1637,
who first learned of the special regard in which the natives
of Zapopan held the image. In 1653, after careful investigation of the facts, the Bishop of Guadalajara, Don Juan Ruiz
Colmenero, issued a decretal declaring the image "miraculous" and appointing the eighteenth of December as the annual
celebration of the Feast of Our Lady of the Expectation of
Zapopan. Under this title the image is still venerated today.

There are other titles of Our Lady of Zapopan for which
she is justly celebrated. These are: Patroness of Guadalajara,
General of the Armies, and Queen of Jalisco. Each of the
three has its proper history.

The end of the seventeenth century saw Guadalajara
scourged by a terrible epidemic. The Bishop ordered the statue

of Our Lady of Zapopan to be carried in procession from its temple into the cathedral of Guadalajara. There is in the ecclesiastical archives a sworn testimonial from the medical profession in Guadalajara, certifying that, following this procession, the plague ceased at once. In 1721, with the onslaught of another plague, Our Lady's image was again brought to Guadalajara and carried from one barrio to another, again effecting a cessation of the plague. Our Lady was also invoked for protection against the violent storms and lightning which threaten Guadalajara during the rainy season.

For these and other reasons Our Lady of Zapopan was officially declared Patroness of Guadalajara specifically "against storms, lightning, and epidemics." Accordingly, each year from 1734 up to the present day, Our Lady of Zapopan leaves her sanctuary on the thirteenth of June and all through the rainy season, until the fourth of October, visits the churches in every barrio of Guadalajara.

In 1821, the "Year of Independence," the achievement of independence took place on the thirteenth of June, at the time Our Lady's image was entering Guadalajara for her annual pilgrimage. Accordingly the government of Jalisco decided to commission Our Lady of Zapopan "General of the Army of the State." On the fifteenth of September in that year, in the presence of the officials of both Church and State, the venerable image was vested in the blue shoulder sash and gold baston of a general. In 1852, while Guadalajara was in a state of siege, with the water supply of the city cut off, General Blancarte placed a new sash of rank on Our Lady of Zapopan and had a twenty-one-gun salute fired in her honor, reinvoking her as Patroness and General of the army of Jalisco. Once again the Virgin effectively protected her city. In 1894 the Governor of Jalisco made a similar proclamation, and bestowed a new sash upon the image.

In the year 1919 Our Lady of Zapopan received a new honor, this time from the Vatican. On the seventeenth of June in that year, the Vatican Chapter decreed the canonical Coronation of Our Lady of Zapopan. The sacred image was solemnly invested with a golden crown in the cathedral of Guadalajara.

Another honor came to Our Lady of Zapopan on the tenth of January, 1940, when His Holiness Pope Pius XII raised the sanctuary in Zapopan to the rank of a minor basilica.

If one wishes to see Our Lady of Zapopan in her own basilica, one must visit her between the fifth of October and the thirteenth of June, the time of the dry season in Jalisco. During the rainy season, about four months out of the year, the Patroness and Queen of Jalisco goes to visit her subjects in the capital city of Guadalajara. Dressed in her traveling clothes, the medieval pilgrim's cloak and broad-brimmed hat, she looks like one of the pilgrims in an early woodcut of Chaucer's *Canterbury Tales*. Her royal progress from one parish to another in the capital is marked by all the pomp and medieval pageantry one usually associates with the European court of an earlier century. On the Blessed Virgin's triumphal journey she is accompanied at all times by the famous "Guard of Our Lady of Zapopan," an honor society, membership in which is a jealously coveted privilege. In their brilliantly striped uniforms, metal helmets, pikestaffs and swords, these troops remind one of the Swiss Guard of the Vatican.

During the royal visitation to the parishes of Guadalajara, the *filigreses* of each church strive to outdo one another in rendering homage to their Queen, and it may truly be said that Guadalajara is in a state of continual *fiesta*.

But if the months when Our Lady goes to Guadalajara cause a universal rejoicing in the capital, her return to Zapopan can only be described as a veritable triumph. On the fifth of October, after a Solemn Mass celebrated in the cathedral of Guadalajara, Our Lady is borne back to the basilica of Zapopan in the arms of the Archbishop. Guadalajara turns out to bid her adieu and to accompany her to her royal palace. The stately procession includes a line of cars that stretches from the cathedral of Guadalajara to the basilica of Zapopan. Overhead airplanes strew flowers along the line of march. From many thousands of throats the air is filled with stirring hymns, so as almost to drown out the military bands which accompany the procession. In the broad courtyard of the basilica, gaily dressed and befeathered groups of Indian dancers from faraway villages in other parts of Mexico add their strange and exotic rhythms and chants in a dozen tongues. Far into the night, fireworks, lights, and music attest the joy of the *jaliscenses* at their Monarch's triumphal homecoming.

The visitor is fortunate who can arrange to come to Zapopan on the fifth of October. Or you may try to visit Our Lady of Zapopan on the eighteenth of December, her titular feast, or on the eighteenth of January, anniversary of her Pontifical Coronation. But whether you visit Our Lady of Zapopan on one of these days, on another of her feasts, or, in fact, on any day of the year, you will come away convinced that the Faith is very much alive in Mexico — Land of Mary's Wonders.

XVI

NUESTRA SEÑORA DE LOS DOLORES DE SORIANO

(OUR LADY OF SORROWS)

Soriano, Querétaro

*Y*OU will not find Soriano mentioned in the touring maps, nor in the conventional guidebook on Mexico, for that matter. And after all, it is just a short stretch on a rough road, often hardly more than a rocky trail, through a section of the Sierra Gorda. A handful of poor dwellings huddles together as if for companionship amid the desolation, and there is a sprinkling of mean little *tiendas* which sell necessities and small luxuries . . . and one thing more.

Even the adventurous traveler may be deterred by the spectacle of the monotonous plain, scarcely broken from time to time by the first tentative counterforts of the Sierra Gorda. Suddenly, to his pleasure and astonishment, a broad plateau raises itself somewhat above the level of the terrain. On this plateau, giving shade and, as it were, protection to an ancient little chapel and the handful of poor dwellings huddled before it, stands a majestic church. Such is the pueblo of Soriano.

"Am I imagining?" the traveler asks himself. "What possible reason for an edifice of such magnificence in this sleepy little place?"

But when the traveler enters the church, and standing just inside the atrium, gazes down the sun-filled nave to the beautifully proportioned sanctuary, he will have his answer.

OUR LADY OF SORROWS

Soriano, Querétaro

Raised above the altar upon a simple pedestal, stands an image serene and full of majesty — the miraculous image of Our Lady of Sorrows of Soriano.

This little image, for it is only twenty-six inches high, is a model of beauty and grace. The lifelike human lineaments do not detract from the spiritual character — nor does the expression of sorrow, deep beyond the telling. In her features, the regal dignity of the sovereign and the intense suffering of the mother are marvelously blended. The hands too, with their fingers interlaced before the breast, reflect the anguish which rends the maternal heart. And the physical marks upon the features bear witness to a history that was not always peaceful. For the image of Our Lady of Sorrows, like her whom it represents, has had more than an ordinary share of trials, as we shall see.

The deep and lively devotion of the early Franciscan missionaries to the Blessed Virgin is well known. As they journeyed through the remotest parts of New Spain, these intrepid men left along their trail almost innumerable images of Our Lady. Under one or other of her glorious titles, these images served as a focal point for the devotions of the neophyte Christians. Their presence gave, as it were, warmth and light to the new dwelling places of the religion of the Cross. Just as a mother's presence brightens and enlivens the home, so did the presence of Mary, the Mother of Jesus, bring to the cold and cheerless pagan hearth the light and warmth of her maternal love. More than once, Mary was the mystical force which conquered the recalcitrant will of some rude Indian tribe, subduing the hearts to the lightsome burden and sweet yoke of the Divine Master of souls.

It must have been one of these apostolic men of the cord and cowl who enshrined, in a primitive chapel in Maconí, the venerated image of Our Lady of Sorrows. History has not left us his name, nor the date of his labors in this rude corner of the Sierra Gorda. But we can affirm that the pueblo of Maconí was probably evangelized by the Franciscans about the middle of the sixteenth century, even though its official foundation did not take place until 1635, when Fernández de Tovar took possession of it for the Spanish Crown.

Perhaps the first missionary to preach to the Indians of Maconí was Fray Alonso Rangel. The historian Mendieta says of this intrepid Franciscan that "he came to New Spain in the year 1529. He was the first to learn the Otomie tongue, and preached in this language the word of God in the provinces of Jilotepec, Tula, and their environs. There he converted a great number of people to the Faith of the Lord Jesus Christ. He baptized them, and destroyed all their idols at great peril to his life, because their priests could not stand to see their false gods burned."

Some ancient legends from the district around Maconí, even though their historicity may not be verified with certainty, at least serve to verify the antiquity of the tradition of Our Lady's image. One charming little legend is the story of the "Little Shepherdess."

Many years ago in Maconí, a little Indian girl was guarding her family's flock of sheep. Through the night she tended them, and in the morning sought a new field for grazing. One morning, as she was driving the sheep to graze upon the sparse grass of that rocky and arid region, another young girl of about her own age appeared.

"Come and play with me," invited the young stranger.

"Oh, but I can't!" replied the little shepherdess. "I must take our sheep to find grass and water. My parents would be very angry if I were to leave them."

The strange girl smiled.

"Do not be afraid," she said. "Today your sheep will find water and grass without you, and more than ever before. Come and play!"

The young Indian child felt the assurance in the other's voice, and believed her new friend. So the two maidens played games, while the sheep wandered off untended.

From the doorway of their rough *jacal,* the parents of the maid saw their sheep grazing unguarded. They went out looking for their daughter, and found her some distance from the flock, apparently unconcerned about its welfare. They began to upbraid the child for neglecting her charge.

"But there is no need to fear," the little shepherdess assured them. "The sheep are well provided with grass and water, and nothing will happen to them."

"That is a strange way to talk," replied her father. "And how do you know that the sheep are well provided, when you no longer guard them?"

"I am certain, Papa," the child answered, "because my little playmate told me so, and she always knows what is right."

"Playmate?" said her parents. "But there are no children of your age in the district. Who is this playmate?"

Following the road pointed out by their daughter, the Indian couple came to a hidden site. There they found a beautiful image of Our Lady of Sorrows. They erected on the spot a simple shrine, placed the Virgin therein, and began to venerate her. This legend serves to show that the origin of the image of Our Lady among the people of Maconí is shrouded in the mists of their Christian beginnings.

The early cult of Our Lady of Sorrows at Maconí, and the ancient presence of her image there, is evidenced by another fact. A stream flows along the burial ground, or *campo santo,* of Maconí, at a distance of about one hundred yards. (This may be the ancient Arroyo del Coní, from which the

pueblo takes its name.) Halfway across this stream stands a
huge rock, upon which can still be seen, though now scarcely
discernible, the faint outlines of the image of Our Lady.
Every year on Good Friday the natives of the region gather
here, bringing flowers and singing their ancient hymns, and
invoking the intercession of Our Lady through the image engraved in rock. It is as though Mary wanted to leave here,
in this remote and primitive place, a memory of the time when
the inhabitants offered her their prayers and their hearts. In
fact, the inhabitants preserve there an uninterrupted tradition
of the cult of Our Lady of Sorrows.

How the image of Our Lady of Sorrows came from her
ancient home in Maconí to her present one in Soriano is the
second, and not the least interesting, part of our story.

Once the epoch of the Conquistadors had passed, very few,
unfortunately, are the records kept of the beginnings of a new
form of civilization in Mexico. The life and customs of the
Indians were changed in many ways; so was their religious
outlook. As a result, the fierce intertribal wars, with all their
degrading and debilitating effects, virtually disappeared. Under
the apostolic influence of the first missionaries, Franciscans,
Dominicans, and others, the natives willingly embraced the
Catholic Faith. It is true that at times their lot was not ma-
terially altered, but they enjoyed at least, under the aegis of
Holy Mother Church, that peace of conscience that comes
with living according to the Divine Law. Only occasionally
did something happen to disturb that tranquillity. From time
to time, however, the nomadic tribes from the north, aided
by their semi-barbarous allies from the mountain fastnesses
of central Mexico, swept down upon the little Christian communities. At such times the blackened ruins of smouldering
buildings alone would remain to tell the tale.

Fray Francisco Palou, that tireless Franciscan missionary, mentions this region and its natives in his book on the life and work of another great Franciscan, his companion and friend, Fray Junipero Serra:

"It begins about thirty leagues distance from the city of Querétaro and extends a hundred leagues in length, and thirty in width. In its scrub lands live the Indians of the Pame Nation, completely wild, in spite of being surrounded by Christian peoples."

The Pame were among the tribes who had never submitted themselves completely to the authority of the Spanish Crown, nor accepted the teachings of Christianity in their entirety. The harsh and mountainous terrain lent itself ideally to the manner of life of these Chichimeca marauders. Swooping down from their mountain fastnesses upon peaceful settlements, they would leave the buildings completely destroyed and the inhabitants slaughtered. On one such raid, of whose exact date we are not certain, they fell upon the little mission at Maconí, leaving the church burned to the ground.

This was a sorrowful period in the history of the missions. We can safely assert that in the Sierra Gorda, between 1715 and 1740, no Spaniard or Christian Indian was safe. According to the nineteenth-century writer Peña: "In this period nothing remained in the Sierra to recall the dominion of Spain, nor even Christian civilization, for the missions were burnt, the missionaries were sacrificed at the hands of the insurgent Indians, and the towns, which were raised up in the shadow of the Cross and under the protection of those self-sacrificing priests, completely disappeared."

In those troubled times, with the scarcity of soldiers and missionaries, and the indefensible nature of the terrain, no effort was made to restore Maconí. So the ruins of the little church remained neglected and almost forgotten, for no one

knows exactly how many years. And hidden beneath the
rubble lay the image of Our Lady of Sorrows.

In 1723, with the discovery of new mines in the vicinity,
the pueblo of El Doctor began to repopulate, and by 1774
it had become an independent parish with its own pastor. One
of the missions attended from El Doctor was Maconí. During
this period El Doctor received the religious ministrations of a
zealous missionary Franciscan, Fray Guadalupe Soriano. This
apostolic *fraile,* exercising his pastoral ministry, ranged far
and wide into the remotest corners of that section of the Sierra
Gorda, as the secular and ecclesiastical archives testify. The
natives of the Villa de Colón still relate the following tale
concerning him.

At one time, Fray Guadalupe Soriano, accompanied by an
Indian helper, traveled to Maconí, for the spiritual ministra-
tion of the inhabitants. The pueblo still bore eloquent and
tragic witness to the disastrous Chichimeca massacre many
years before. When Padre Soriano inquired of the natives how
the church came to be so completely destroyed, they replied,

"Padre, those evil Indians filled the church with great loads
of kindling wood, and set fire to it."

While his Indian guide was preparing their simple meal,
the apostolic Franciscan went to see the remains of the ancient
chapel. Poking around in the ruins, he caught the glint of a
metallic object shining amid the rubble. Moved by curiosity,
he began to remove the heap of stone and charred wood. To
his amazement, there appeared the head of an image of Our
Lady. Calling upon some of the natives to help him, the
Padre at length uncovered with their aid the statue of Our
Lady of Sorrows. In some unexplained manner, it had fallen
beneath a huge block of stone, which had protected it both
from the falling timbers and from the fire. What was equally
important, the protected situation of the image had kept it

safe those many years from the destructive forces of the elements. Aside from some minor burns on the face, the image
had been preserved without suffering any observable deterioration.

When Padre Soriano left the pueblo of Maconí, he was
carrying the precious image. Desirous of enshrining it in a
place where it would be suitably cared for and honored, he
took the statue to the mission of Santo Domingo; later this
became known as Santo Domingo de Soriano, and in our own
times, Soriano. There the image remains to this day, in the
Church of Santo Domingo.

In 1744, when Escandón came to the Sierra Gorda, he
found the Dominican Fathers in charge. At that time the
mission consisted of seven Spanish families, seven families of
Otomies, six of whom had helped to found the mission, and
forty-eight families of Chichimecas. A relic of those early
Dominicans still remains, in the little wooden church that
served for a time to house the image found by Fray Guadalupe
Soriano. Later the mission came under the charge of the
Franciscans in Tolimanejo. Finally in 1748, Archbishop Rubío
y Salinas erected the mission into a parochial church. At the
present day San Francisco Tolimanejo and Santo Domingo
de Soriano are united into the Villa de Colón, with municipal
administration on the site of the former Tolimanejo, now
Colón. The parish church is at Colón; and Soriano, with its
Church of Santo Domingo, has become the mission church.

The pilgrim who wishes to make a *romería* to this shrine
should try to arrive there for Friday of Passion Week — the
Feast of the Seven Dolors of Our Lady. This is the principal
feast of the shrine, and each year it is celebrated with great
solemnity. As early as the Monday of Passion Week, huge
numbers of the faithful begin to arrive. Thursday and Friday,
the latter the actual day of Our Lady's feast, the rough roads

are crowded with pilgrims who have been traveling, some of them, for three or more days. It has been estimated that on the eve and on the feast day alone, between fifteen and twenty thousand *romeros* come to Soriano.

For days before, there is tremendous bustling and activity, as the small merchants and the peripatetic vendors arrive with their wares. A minor miracle in the commercial life of the pueblo is accomplished. For this little hamlet, which can boast of but a handful of poor *tiendas,* suddenly blossoms out with hundreds of gay *puestos,* or booths, all doing a thriving business. Indeed, many of the merchants completely dispose of their stock before the *fiesta* is over. The whole scene presents an animated canvas of gay colors.

And of course there are *cohetes* (skyrockets) brought by various pilgrim societies, often from great distances and always in astonishing supply. In fact, it has been estimated that between one hundred thousand and one hundred and fifty thousand *cohetes* are shot off during the *fiesta!* In addition, a huge *castillo,* a kind of progressive pinwheel and rocket assembly in one, is brought from Querétaro and erected to serve as the *pièce de résistance* of the fireworks display on Friday night.

But the religious character is foremost in the *fiesta.* On Thursday, a Solemn Mass is celebrated and a distinguished preacher brought in for the occasion. On Friday another Solemn Mass is sung, and the preacher, usually from Querétaro, delivers a panegyric on Our Blessed Lady. Following the Mass, the image of Our Lady of Sorrows is carried in solemn procession through the church, and finally taken to bless the pueblo of Soriano. Then the sacred image is placed at the Communion rail, where all through the day and far into the evening, streams of pilgrims press forward to kiss her garments.

The people of Soriano and of the surrounding countryside in the Sierra Gorda have a deep love and devotion for Mary.

the Mother of Sorrows. And Our Lady, on the other hand, has rewarded that devotion by granting innumerable benefits to her clients. Ample proof of their gratitude is shown by the multitude of thank-offerings in the parish church of Soriano. Hundreds of paintings, photos, cards, letters of thanks, picture-stories of cures, and silver and gold *milagros* adorn the walls of the old chapel next to the present-day sanctuary.

Among the many favors granted through the intercession of Our Lady of Sorrows of Soriano, the following have been chosen as representative, and because they have been officially verified. I call them, respectively, "The Young Seamstress" and "The Conscientious Deserter."

The first story concerns a young lady named Elvira, very pious and very poor, who worked as a seamstress in Mexico City. She was gravely stricken with a tumor. "We shall have to operate at once," said the physicians.

A friend of her mother heard the news. "You must pray for your daughter to Our Lady of Sorrows of Soriano," she counseled. "She works great miracles."

Elvira's mother followed the advice of her friend. She prayed earnestly to the Virgin for her daughter's health. The next day, the one scheduled for the operation, the young girl awoke, well and sound. Soon the surgeon arrived to prepare for the operation.

"But I feel perfectly well now," said Elvira. "There is no need for an operation."

The skeptical surgeon made a careful medical examination.

"The girl has no tumor now," he announced at last to the mother. "What medicine has she taken, and who prescribed it?"

"There was no medicine," replied the mother. "I prayed to Our Lady of Sorrows of Soriano, asking the Virgin to cure my daughter. I promised, if she were cured, to visit Our Lady's shrine and give a thank-offering."

"A remarkable story," said the man of science. "All I can certify is that the young lady was suffering from a malignant tumor a few days ago, and that today she is perfectly well."

But Elvira's mother knew who had cured her child, and when mother and daughter made a pilgrimage to Soriano, one September day not many years ago, their hearts were full of gratitude to Our Lady of Sorrows.

Another remarkable story of Our Lady's intercession I have called "The Case of the Conscientious Deserter." In 1941 a letter arrived at the shrine from a lady in Mexico City, who enclosed a substantial alms, and related the following tale:

During the time when Venustiano Carranza was at the height of his lawless career, the lady's father was impressed into the *Carrancista* troops. Disgusted by the depredations of these *pistoleros,* he watched his opportunity and deserted. Some time later these same *pistoleros* captured him, and he was sentenced to death by firing squad. The squad had already been drawn up, and the unfortunate man placed before it, when he recommended his cause to Our Lady of Sorrows of Soriano. The officer in charge prepared to order "Fire!" At that moment an official came running into the courtyard with an order halting the execution. The conscientious deserter had just received a pardon! The sworn testimony of the old soldier's daughter is on record, a grateful memorial to the miraculous intervention of Our Lady on behalf of one of her children.

OUR LADY OF SANTA ANITA
Santa Anita, Jalisco

XVII

NUESTRA SEÑORA DE SANTA ANITA

(OUR LADY OF SANTA ANITA)

Santa Anita, Jalisco

ALMOST before he knows it, the traveler on the way from Guadalajara to Lake Chapala will have passed the signpost for Santa Anita, a few miles out of Guadalajara. A dirt road, more suited to horseback or burro than to the modern automobile, leads off the highway to the southeast. But the more adventurous, whether devout pilgrim or merely curious tourist, will be richly repaid for the mile and a half of rather rough going which takes him to the little pueblo of Santa Anita. For here, in the parish church attached to a convent of Franciscan friars, is venerated the legendary and miraculous image of Our Lady of the Purification.

In ancient times, Santa Anita was called Atlixtac ("White Water"), after a local spring colored by the whitish clay of that region. Certain Indians founded a settlement there in 1519, by license from the King of Tonalá, as a reward for their efforts in resisting the Tarascan invasion from Michoacán in 1510. When Cortés' lieutenant, Nuño de Guzmán, conquered Tonalá in 1530, the native chieftains received baptism. Two Franciscans, Fray Juan de Padilla and Fray Juan de Badillo, accompanied the forces of de Guzmán and first preached the Faith to the Atlixtac Indians.

103

After the Mixton War in 1531, to discourage further up-
risings, Francisco de Bobadilla uprooted the Indian community
of Apozol and settled them in Atlixtac. An early Franciscan
historian, Fray Francisco M. de Torres, chronicles this second
foundation:

"In the year 1542, by order of Miguel de Ibarra, Captain
and chief officer of the Villa of Guadalajara, Santa Ana
Atlixtac was founded by the distinguished Señor Cristobal de
Oñate, Governor of Nueva Galicia. Given at Acatic on the
second day of October."

The Indians took as the Patron of their pueblo Santa Ana;
hence the name Santa Ana Atlixtac. Until 1551 the pueblo
was served by Franciscans from Guadalajara; then, until
1741, it was a *visita* (mission without a resident friar) of the
Franciscans at Tlajomulco. A royal letter patent of Carlos III
in 1784 erected the Franciscan community in Atlixtac into a
permanent convent, still in use today. In 1944 the Archbishop
of Guadalajara, Dr. Don José Garibi Rivera, gave the parish
in perpetuity to the Franciscan Order.

Adjoining the convent is a fine old church of quarrystone
in Churrigueresque style. Within this church is the celebrated
image of Our Lady of the Purification (or *Candelaria*). The
natives of the pueblo have changed its name from Santa Ana
to the affectionate diminutive "Santa Anita." Hence the image
is known as Our Lady of Santa Anita.

Tradition dating before the year 1700 relates the origins
of the image. It was brought to Atlixtac by a hermit, who
came from Europe collecting alms, by royal license, for this
image of Our Lady. The old man fell ill in Atlixtac, and a
Christian Indian woman, Agustina, took him into her home
and cared for him. On his deathbed, the hermit entrusted the
image to Agustina. She held it in great veneration, and even

hid it away, fearing that the authorities might take it from her. Soon the Virgin began to grant signal favors to the people.

Many legends are told of Agustina, the local *curandera* (native doctor). When called in, she first urged the sick person to have devotion to, and confidence in, the Mother of God. Returned home after treating the sick one, Agustina would light a tallow candle before Our Lady's image, and, while praying for the health of her patient, would carefully observe the features of the image. If the face became bright and glowing, Agustina knew that the patient would recover. Then she would invoke the Virgin and anoint the sick person with tallow from her votive candle. The patient would recover. If, however, the features of the Virgin became dark, it was a sign that the illness was mortal. In that case Agustina would announce the imminence of death, exhorting the patient at the same time to receive the Sacraments and to prepare for a holy demise.

Soon the Franciscans at Tlajomulco learned of the prophetic image, and questioned Agustina. She freely declared that the varying aspects of the face of the image were the key to her uncanny knack in prognosticating health or death. The *frailes* made a test of the image, bearing it to their convent at Tlajomulco, to one of their number who was gravely ill. As the image was brought into his cell, according to tradition, the sick religious exclaimed:

"You are very beautiful, O Lady, but very dark." And shortly he died a holy death.

When Agustina died, the Indians placed the image in the chapel of the Hospital of the Immaculate Conception, which still stands, now known as the Sanctuary of Our Lady of Guadalupe. Little by little devotion to Our Lady's image diminished, and in the course of the years it became wholly neglected.

Some time after the middle of the seventeenth century, the Franciscan Fray Ignacio Tellez, on a visit from Tlajomulco, happened to see the image, its vestments old and torn and covered with dust. Inquiring among the oldest inhabitants, he learned that it was the miraculous image to which, in former times, the Franciscans as well as the Indians had had great devotion. Fray Tellez caused the statue to be vested in new garments, and resolved to foster anew the ancient devotion to Our Lady. He began another sanctuary directly opposite the old chapel, laying the first stone on the Feast of the Assumption of Our Lady, August the fifteenth, 1700.

In his sermon at the dedication, Fray Nicolás de Ornelas Mendoza y Valdivia, Chronicler of the Franciscan Province of Jalisco, had a brand-new marvel to relate. In the congregation was a lady from the distinguished Segovia family of Guadalajara. While this lady was being assisted from her horse, the animal became frightened and bolted; and its mistress, whose heel had been caught in the stirrup, was dragged along beneath its hoofs. This was a common accident in those times, and ordinarily resulted in death or crippling injuries to the victim. But the Señora had the presence of mind to call out to the Virgin of Santa Anita. Immediately her foot came free of the stirrup and the animal jumped away, leaving her unharmed. Fray Nicolás also mentioned the case of Fray José Núñez, Guardian of the convent of Tlajomulco, who was cured of a long illness accompanied by high fevers, through Our Lady's intercession. Fray Núñez made the Sign of the Cross upon his breast with oil from the lamp burning before the image of Our Lady; immediately the fever left him and he rose from his cot, completely recovered.

In 1918, when a terrible epidemic of influenza swept through the United States and Mexico, Santa Anita was severely stricken. Our Lady of Santa Anita was carried in solemn procession through the streets of the pueblo, and the epidemic was halted. The following day two persons died who had been stricken some time before. Not another death from influenza was recorded. Because of her signal intercession, Our Lady of Santa Anita is now also called *Abogada de los Infermos* ("Help of the Sick"). Today the venerable image reposes in a sanctuary begun in 1732 and completed in 1807.

Our Lady of Santa Anita is a small wooden sculpture, a foot and a half high, of Spanish origin, painted over gilt by the process known as *estofo*. The tunic is of opaque vermilion and the mantle of sea-green enamel. Centuries of being vested by hands more zealous than skilled had left the upper half of the statue much the worse for wear, and shortly after 1918, the figure was restored by a competent and reverent artist. The face is rather narrower than oval. The features are of extreme delicacy, the nose small and aquiline, the eyes olive-green, large, and finely delineated.

At times Our Lady of Santa Anita is vested in cloth of gold or silver; at other times all in white, richly bordered in gold, silver and jewel work, the braid, fringes, and tassels being of gold. In her right hand she holds a golden candlestick with a small candle, and on her left arm the Child Jesus, as richly vested as His Mother. The Child wears upon His head a little golden imperial crown set with pearls.

The Virgin Mother wears the imperial crown of gold set with fine jewels, and around her head is the stylized aureole, gold over silver. Devout clients have given her golden earrings and collars of pearl. The platform upon which she stands is of antique silver, and beneath her feet is a half-moon of silver capped at the points by a star.

In former times the *fiesta* of Our Lady of Santa Anita was celebrated on the fifteenth of August, the Feast of the

Assumption. This day was selected in a manner that recalls Old Testament days, or the *auspices* of the Roman soothsayers. Fray Ignacio Tellez, whom we have mentioned previously, wrote out separately all the Mysteries, or principal feasts, of Our Lady. Lots were then drawn, and the choice fell upon the Mystery of the Assumption. For over a hundred years after that time, the Feast of Our Lady of Santa Anita was celebrated on the fifteenth of August. But since the image is that of Our Lady of *Candelaria,* or the Purification, the celebration should properly come on the second of February, Mary's feast under that title in the universal Church. Accordingly in the year 1782, Fray José Patiño changed the celebration to the second of February, and thus it has remained to the present.

Each year the *fiesta* is celebrated with great solemnity and rejoicing. The Franciscan Fathers at Santa Anita dedicate a solemn novena which closes on the feast day itself. Every day of the novena there is Solemn Mass, a sermon by one of the Franciscans, Benediction of the Most Blessed Sacrament, along with the prayers of the novena. Individual pilgrims and organized *romerías* come into Santa Anita from outlying districts, and, of course, there are fireworks and music in the little plaza.

We may fittingly bring to a close the story of this revered image with a *cuento* from one of the Franciscan *padres.* He told me this tale one evening at sundown, sitting in my little guest room in the convent in Durango, and that is how I came to visit Santa Anita, hundreds of miles away.

According to tradition, Our Lady of Santa Anita notifies the *frailes* of the Franciscan convent there when the time for their death is near. Some years ago, a Franciscan Brother, an old man who had given his life to service in the Order, was very ill. The *padres* were gathered together in the common room talking, when of a sudden there was a sound from the sanctuary as of glass breaking. They rushed into the church and looked about carefully, but could find nothing amiss. They returned to their recreation, and shortly the sound was repeated. Thinking that the glass case protecting the image of Our Lady had broken, they again hastened to the sanctuary, but found everything in order. A third time the incident occurred, with the same result. Then the Father Guardian spoke:

"My Brothers, I believe that Our Lady wants to tell us something," he said. "Evidently one of the community is going to die."

"Perhaps we should tell Brother X —," said another.

And so the *frailes* went to the little cell where the old Brother lay. With tears in their eyes they watched the wasted frame of the faithful follower of Saint Francis, as his gnarled fingers lovingly told the beads of his rosary.

"Brother," said the Father Guardian, "I have a message for you from Our Lady."

"I know," replied the old man. "I am going to die. Just a few minutes ago Our Lady knocked on the door three times, to tell me."

XVIII

NUESTRA SEÑORA DE LOS REMEDIOS DE ZITÁCUARO

(OUR LADY OF THE REMEDIES)

Zitácuaro, Michoacán

SIXTY-SIX hundred feet above sea level, and about half-way between Toluca and Morelia, at the hundred mile mark, stands Zitácuaro. Today a city of over twenty thousand, it was early colonized by the Spaniards and converted to the Faith by the missionary Franciscans. There was a church there at least by the year 1543, barely a generation after Cortés' conquest of Mexico, and at that time it was known as *La Villa de San Juan Tzitácuaro, Provincia y Obispado de Michoacán.* Today, with its charming and unspoiled native markets, and abundance of colorful and picturesque local products, Zitácuaro is a real "find" for the tourist who wants something more than the perfunctory, kaleidoscopic glimpse of Mexico given by the conventional guided tour. And for the devout pilgrim who sees Mexico as "The Land of Mary's Wonders," Zitácuaro is a shining jewel in the diadem of Our Lady's Mexican crown, and one of the palaces where our Queen delights to dwell. For enthroned in the parochial church of this town, there is the wonder-working image of *Nuestra Señora de los Remedios.*

As far as the writer knows, the earliest official account of this image was written by the Fray Alonso Larrea in the Fran-

110

R . de Nª Sª. de los Remedios. que se venera en el Combento de N.
Francisco de la Villa de Sⁿ Juan Zilaquaro. Bendita y alabaq
ª Imaculada Concepsion, de la Beatissima Virgen Maria SS
A devocion del P. F. Felipe Velasco.
ylveria se an 1758

OUR LADY OF THE REMEDIES

Zitácuaro, Michoacán

ciscan Chronicles of the year 1640. Our information here is largely based on a reimpression of a work published in 1749 by Fray Felipe Velasco. The photograph shown is of the woodcut impression in the 1762 edition. The church was then attached to, and in charge of, the Franciscan convent in Zitácuaro. The story might have come straight out of the pages of the *Golden Legend* of Jacobus de Voragine.

When Juan Velásquez de Salazar came from the Kingdom of Castille in Spain to assume jurisdiction, by royal grant, of the encomienda of Tajimaroa, he brought with him this image of Our Lady, intending to keep her in his home, as confidante and adviser of his problems. The long journey from the port of Veracruz was made by the family and retainers on horseback, with all the household goods and other necessities transported by a train of pack mules. One of the mules carried the image, well protected in a sturdy case. The sight of a Spanish hidalgo and *encomendero* traveling to take possession of his holdings must have been quite a sight, and as they passed through the pueblo of Zitácuaro everyone turned out to look. What a cloud of dust the great pack train must have raised! What excitement and shouting among the *arrieros* (muleteers) as they busily plied their whips and sharp wooden goads to keep the recalcitrant mules from straying out of line or falling behind!

While being driven through the plaza, amid the dust and the shouting, one of the mules, the one carrying the sacred image, suddenly bolted out of line and into the patio before the church. Straight to the portals of the church it ran, and then stood still. With blows and oaths and tuggings upon the lead rope, the *arrieros* attempted to get the animal back into the train. To no avail; the mule stood as if rooted in the ground. The situation caused great interest among the bystanders, and their interest turned to a devout excitement when

they learned the contents of the case. Running to the head
of the column, they told the *encomendero* what had happened,
begging him to leave the image in Zitácuaro.

When Don Juan Velásquez heard the tale, he knew that
it was Our Lady's will to remain in the pueblo. Not only did
he agree to leave the image there, but also he gave a substantial offering to build her a permanent tabernacle. When
the *arrieros* removed the case and placed it on the ground, the
mule fell on its knees before the Virgin, as if to signify the reverence due to the Mother of God. A report of the prodigy
quickly spread throughout the region, and soon pious visitors
were traveling from far and wide, to honor Our Lady's image,
and to invoke her in their needs.

One of those who came to offer homage was the saintly
Fray Francisco de Castro. Devoutly he prayed to the Mother
of God before her image, opening his heart. When it was
time to leave, so runs the tradition, he decided to take the
image back to his convent, as its present temple was small and
poorly constructed. He took the measurements of the statue
and ordered a case to be made for it. But when the image
was taken down from the altar and placed in the box, it was
found that the receptacle was too small by a depth of three
fingers. Calling in one of the officials, the friar again carefully
took the measurements in his presence, and ordered a larger
box to be built. This was done, but upon trial they discovered
that a second time the case was too small by the depth of three
fingers. Attempting to force the cover down upon the image,
the workmen injured one of the eyebrows and the tip of the
nose. As late as the year 1762 one could still observe the
damage done to the features by this remarkable circumstance.
After some reflection, Fray Francisco understood that it was
Mary's will to leave her image in the church, and modified
his own desires accordingly.

The people of Zitácuaro determined to build for their Queen a splendid new church to replace the small, decaying structure of adobe. At that time there lived in the mining town of Zacualpa a certain Manuel de Santa Cruz, who had lost his revenues and means of livelihood. To escape his creditors and the shame of prison, Manuel decided to leave his wife and children and strike out elsewhere to make his fortune. On the way he promised to offer several novenas to Our Lady of Los Remedios and to place his fortunes under her protection. So he went to the church, offered the novenas to Mary, along with his necessities, and then began his journey. But suddenly he was seized with an overpowering desire to see his wife and children once more, and so resolved to visit them secretly. By a little-used path Manuel was making his way back to Zacualpa, when suddenly an Indian stood before him.

"Adiós, Don Manuel," the stranger greeted him. "Where are you going?"

"This is very strange!" thought Manuel. "I have never seen this Indian in my life, and yet he greets me by name."

"You know my name, *hijo,*" Manuel replied. "How is that?"

"When I was a *mozo,* I had the honor of serving you," said the Indian.

Now Don Manuel had never before set eyes on the man; of that he was certain.

"Then you must be my guardian angel," he retorted, "for this is the first time I have seen your face."

"Señor," the man answered, "you seem *muy triste* — sad about something. Perhaps I can be of service to you."

Manuel looked at the other carefully, and saw only a poor native who, it seemed clear, had nothing but the shabby clothes on his back. The Spaniard was accustomed to judge by appearances, and so he said:

"The help I need, you cannot give."

"But *Señor*," persisted the stranger, "you are in trouble; that I can tell. Won't you let me help you?"

For some reason, Don Manuel was strangely moved by the interest of this humble creature of God. Then, too, his troubles weighed heavily upon his heart, and there seemed no one on earth to whom he could turn for help. So at length he related to the Indian his financial and domestic worries, adding that he had to leave home because of them.

"Then put your soul at ease, *Señor*," answered the other, when Manuel had finished the tale. "For while I was working in the mines, years ago, I found a rich and hidden vein. If you will come with me, I shall show it to you — but on one condition only."

"By all means!" cried the Spaniard. "Only tell me the condition!"

"It is this, *Señor*. First, you must pay all your debts."

"But certainly!" retorted Manuel. "I am a Spaniard, and a man of honor!"

"Of course, *Señor!* But there is another part to the condition," went on the mysterious native. "After you have paid your debts, you must build a new and beautiful church for *La Virgen de Zitácuaro,* to whom you have been praying."

After Manuel had promised to do this, the Indian led him by unfamiliar paths to the mine of Sultepeque. Pointing to a certain spot, he said:

"Dig here, *Señor,* and before you have gone down one vara, you will find great riches."

With some misgivings, Don Manuel did as he was instructed. Wonder of wonders, before he had dug through three feet of earth, he uncovered a rich vein of silver. Turning to share his good fortune with his benefactor, he found himself alone. To the end of his days, Manuel de Santa Cruz was convinced that Our Lady had sent an angel in human guise to his aid.

Don Manuel went to the City of Mexico and registered his claim with the authorities. He paid his debts. Then mindful of his promise to Our Lady, and thankful too, he built a magnificent stone church, with a fine organ and a magnificent retable. The people of Zitácuaro still talk of this miracle, and of the kindliness and understanding of Our Lady, who preferred that a man first pay his debts of justice, and only then build a house for her.

By this time the miraculous character of the image of the Virgin of Los Remedios had spread far and wide, beyond the boundaries of Michoacán, and scarcely a day passed that some devout and afflicted pilgrim did not arrive to pray before Mary's shrine and beg for succor in his needs. Among these petitioners was one Hipólito Rodríguez, from the mining community of Temascaltepeque. The great sorrow in his life was a crippled daughter, who had been confined to her bed for eight years, and in the care and treatment of whom he had spent his entire savings. Convinced at last that the girl was beyond human aid, the sorrowing father determined to bring her to visit the Virgin. After a long and painful journey, the girl arrived in Zitácuaro, borne on the shoulders of some Indians, and, as it is related, more dead than alive. Carried to the church, she began the nine days of prayer to Our Lady, from her bed. On the third day the young woman was able to sit up unaided; on the sixth, she arose and began to walk a bit. By the last day of the novena, she was in perfect health, and appeared so fresh and lovely that it was difficult for anyone to believe she was the same creature. The deforming effects of her crippling illness had entirely disappeared, and even the memory of it seemed to her merely a dream.

But the story does not end here. A charming sequel with a touch of romance is recorded by the early chroniclers. The fame of this miracle went abroad, and came to the ears of a certain rich and powerful Spaniard, by name Jiménez, who was *síndic* (trustee) of the Convent of San Francisco in Toluca.

"A young woman to whom the Blessed Virgin has granted such a miracle," thought he, "would certainly be an honor to my house and family." And communicating with Señor Rodríguez, he entered into arrangements for a marriage between the young girl and his own son.

But there was a difficulty. The girl's family was very poor, and the pride of Hipólito Rodríguez would not allow him to give his daughter in marriage unless he could provide a suitable dowry.

"Very well," answered Señor Jiménez to the father's objections. "I will provide her with a dowry myself."

And he endowed the *señorita* with a great sum of money. The early chronicler remarks that it seems almost as great a miracle as the former, for the lame girl became healed, and the poor girl rich, through the intercession of Our Lady of Los Remedios. And so they were married; and, we hope, they lived happily ever after.

Another remarkable cure directly attributed to Our Lady of Los Remedios concerns a woman named Jerónima Bautista, severely crippled in one of her arms and in both legs. Medical treatment having proved fruitless, Jerónima came to Zitácuaro to make a novena to Our Lady. She had to be carried up the steps of the church. (Jerónima must have been a woman of ample proportions, by the way, as we read that it took four people to lift her!) She confessed and received Holy Communion on the first day of the novena. The second day she experienced a considerable relief from pain, and on the third day she walked to the church unaided. On the ninth day of the novena the lameness had completely disappeared, and Jerónima walked about the pueblo, telling everyone about her good fortune. After completing the novena and giving heartfelt thanks to Our Lady of Los Remedios, Jerónima set out for her own home. Passing through the pueblo of Tuxpan on the way, she met the Father Guardian and another *fraile* from the convent in Tuxpan, and with great enthusiasm told them of her miraculous cure. It is probable the good friars were a little startled at her exuberant deportment on the occasion. For, to demonstrate the new-found strength of her formerly crippled arm, she picked some oranges from a convenient tree and began shying them across the plaza!

However, the understanding Franciscans evidently found her enthusiasm pardonable, for as a *recuerdo* of the miracle they presented her with a garment used to vest the venerable image of Our Lady. Jerónima guarded the precious relic with due veneration, and often applied it to others in suffering.

The same lady had a slave, a colored woman, who had been devoted to her throughout her crippling illness, and for whom she entertained a great affection. Some time after the remarkable events related above, the slave gave birth to a stillborn child. Moved by the sorrow of the unfortunate mother, Jerónima took the sacred garment of Our Lady and laid it over the dead child, invoking the intercession of *La Virgen de los Remedios*. Shortly the child began to stir, and life flowed into his little body. The baby lived for eight months; long enough, we are sure, for the saving waters of baptism to be poured over him.

And now for a description of the venerable image of Our Lady of Los Remedios of Zitácuaro. The ancient woodcut accompanying this chapter, interesting as it is, can give no idea of the more than passing beauty of the actual figure. Being of Spanish origin, the image is fashioned with great delicacy of feature. It is made of cedar wood, in one piece, and sculptured as far as the waist — the lower portion, as so often in the case of figures designed to be vested, being left in the rough. The color of the features is a light, rosy wheat, with a natural bloom in the cheeks. The eyes are large, well-proportioned and gentle, a soft blue in color; the gracefully arching eyebrows a dusky hazel. The slightly aquiline nose is finely formed, the mouth small, and the delicate lips like the scarlet lace of the Canticle. The rather full face presents an appearance at once majestic and amiable.

At the tip of the nose, the glaze and color have been slightly chipped, and there is a tiny depression, beneath which traces of the plaster priming can be discerned. The left eyebrow also reveals a slight flawing of the glaze and color. Both of these marks are mentioned in the earliest chronicles, written more than three hundred years ago, and bear eloquent testimony to the miracle of the caskets which we have referred to previously. The flowing hair is a light chestnut in color, and appears extraordinarily abundant because of the sculptured tresses beneath. Happily, this does make the appearance less attractive; quite the contrary.

Our Lady of Zitácuaro possesses several rich changes of vestments, lavishly decorated with pearls. She also has many fine jewels, gifts of devout subjects to their Queen. Mary's imperial crown, without which she is never seen, is of gold set with many precious stones. The sovereign figure, about thirty-three inches high, bears in her arms the Divine Child, very small and exquisitely fashioned.

The Mystery, or title, under which Our Lady of Los Remedios of Zitácuaro is venerated, is the Immaculate Conception. Consequently the principal celebration at her shrine takes place on the eighth day of December each year. Today, as for more than three hundred years, the town is crowded with pilgrims, the plaza and streets gay with flags and bunting, and the church alive with lights and color, to do homage to *Nuestra Señora de los Remedios,* Queen of Zitácuaro.

His Holiness Pope Pius XII approved the Pontifical Coronation of Our Lady of Los Remedios, under whose auspices the city of Zitácuaro came into being and under whom it has prospered. The actual coronation with the pontifical crown of gold took place on the twenty-first of November, 1945, with Don Luis Altamirano y Bulnes, Archbishop of Morelia, acting as the delegate of the Supreme Pontiff.

XIX

LA VIRGEN DEL ANILLO

(OUR LADY OF THE RING)

Guadalupe, Zacatecas

$\mathcal{A}$ BOUT four miles southeast of Zacatecas, at the 460-mile mark, stands the little village of Guadalupe. Turning off the highway a few hundred yards, by quaint, old, unpaved streets, the traveler comes to the Franciscan Church and Convent of Our Lady of Guadalupe, named after the renowned shrine and image in Mexico City. The present church dates from the year 1721; the convent was founded in 1707 by that great Franciscan man of God, Fray Antonio Márgil de Jesús. During one hundred and fifty years it was the center of tremendous missionary activity, sending the friars of the Cord and Habit of *Il Poverello* into the furthest reaches of Mexico. In 1859, exclaustration occurred, and the *frailes* were driven from their homes by the antireligious government of the country. Once again in their ancient home, and under the patronage of Our Lady of Guadalupe, they occupy only a small part of the convent, the remainder having been turned into a kind of museum by the Mexican government. Both church and convent play an important part in our story. So does the Venerable Padre Fray Bernardino de Jesús Pérez.

On the eighth of October, 1843, Padre Pérez was elected Guardian of the Apostolic College of Guadalupe. He was a

OUR LADY OF THE RING

Guadalupe, Zacatecas

man renowned for solid virtue, prudence and piety, and beloved by the Franciscan community, who called him affectionately *"Padre Perítoz."* It was during his first term as Guardian that there occurred the memorable events which tradition assigns to the fifteenth of August, 1844.

Soon after Padre Pérez became Guardian of the convent of Guadalupe, two venerable nuns of the Order of Saint Francis began to correspond with him. One was missioned at a convent in Salvatierra; the other, called in religion Madre San Juanita, was in the Convent of San Miguel el Grande. Both wrote that they had received from the Virgin Mary a message ordering them to notify Padre Pérez of a great trial which the Apostolic College of Guadalupe and all the religious there would undergo. Further, he was to assemble all his religious together, and exhort them to obedience to the Holy Rule of Saint Francis, to purity of conscience and to a spirit of fellowship. Further, he was to establish a religious function each year on the fifteenth of August, at which each should confess his faults in choir, and renew his vows in the presence of Our Lady. The Blessed Virgin commanded the Father Guardian, wrote the nuns, to inform his religious that Our Lady desired to be one with the community, and to celebrate with them a spiritual betrothal. To seal the espousals, Our Lady desired that the community present a ring to her image in their chapel; they, in turn, would receive from the Virgin another ring, to remind them of the contract.

Padre Pérez, being a prudent man, spent a great deal of time deliberating upon so grave a matter. In the meantime, the nuns continued to write him, urging him to carry out Our Lady's will. In addition, they declared, the saintly founder of Guadalupe, Fray Antonio Márgil de Jesús, had communicated with them from beyond the grave, urging the religious to carry out Mary's order without delay. To establish the authenticity of these revelations, the two nuns prophesied three signs which Padre Pérez would receive.

First, they told him certain grave and secret things he had been meditating without ever revealing to anyone.

Second, they predicted that Our Lady would shortly preserve him and others from harm during an accident at the convent.

Third, they said that an image in the chapel would be saved from destruction in a mishap, through Our Lady's intercession.

All three predictions came to pass exactly as the nuns had foretold. Padre Pérez had been meditating upon matters which no one else could have even surmised. The hospice caved in one morning when the workmen had finished removing the forms over the vaulting; but despite the large number of people present, including Padre Pérez, no one was injured. On the seventeenth of May, the Feast of Saint Pascal Baylon, during the afternoon hours, the statue of that saint fell from a height of more than fourteen feet; several fingers were damaged, but nothing more.

What went on in the soul of Padre Pérez we can only imagine. By this time there could have been no doubt in his mind regarding the validity of the order from the Queen of Heaven. Shortly thereafter he sent a message to all his absent colleagues, ordering them to return at once to the college, for an important convocation.

Finally the fifteenth of August arrived, the Feast of the Assumption of the Virgin. We may imagine that the celebration, with Solemn Mass and the chanting of the Divine Office, was observed with even more than customary solemnity by the *frailes* of Guadalupe. After the evening procession, the image of *Nuestra Señora del Tránsito,* called by the Franciscans *"La Muertita,"* was placed on its table in the midst of the choir. Following the supper, the Father Guardian called the community together, to their great surprise.

After strictly charging them not to disclose outside of the community of their college what he was about to reveal to them, Padre Perítoz told the assembled religious that he had received a message from heaven. He spoke of the message from their founder, Fray Márgil, exhorting them to live together in charity. Then he revealed to them the special mandate of Our Lady. About a month before, Padre Pérez had ordered a ring to be made, according to the express instruction of the Virgin. He entrusted the work of having the ring fabricated to Don Benito de los Ríos, Trustee of the college.

At this juncture, Padre Pérez showed the ring to his Franciscan community. It was made of gold, upon which was engraved a heart, and around the heart, in Spanish, the following inscription: *"We all offer to thee our hearts and love — for we belong to Mary."*

Padre Pérez went on to say that, when he had the ring made, Our Lady became, as it were, beside herself with anticipation because her sons of Guadalupe were going to render her this homage, and that she spoke to him in the following manner:

"Just as my Son takes His delight with the children of men, and will take it until the end of the world, so do I take my delight, and will take it until the end of the world, with the sons of Francis. I am the ladder by which they go straight to my Most Holy Son; and what they cannot do, I can. And I have to preserve this College until it attains a glorious end. When it was founded, my son Fray Antonio Márgil conveyed it to me in all truth, and I received it under my shield and protection. I desire that those who dwell therein be as angels. . . . "

When they had sung the canticle of the Magnificat and several hymns, the religious confessed their faults, and all renewed their vows. Then Padre Pérez, in the name of the community, placed the ring upon the finger of *"La Muertita"* with the following words:

"My Fathers and Brothers, . . . I, in the name of the Most Holy Virgin, Mother of God and our Mother, promise you eternal life if you will be faithful in the promises which you have made to the Lord, in the vows that you have renewed in His honor; and I promise you all the blessings of heaven, corresponding to your lofty state and office, in the name of the Most Holy Virgin, whose blessing I give you."

All the religious spent the night in prayer before the image of *"La Muertita,"* borne in procession to the chapel of the novitiate. The next day Padre Pérez placed the ring upon the finger of the painting of Our Lady of Guadalupe which rests above the high altar in the chapel.* There it remains to this day, as it appears in the accompanying photograph.

There is a pious legend kept alive among the religious at the Convent of Guadalupe, and told by them to the author. When Padre Pérez went to place the ring upon the hand of Our Lady, the fingers separated to facilitate his action. The unusual angle of the little finger on the left hand of the Virgin, in this painting made many years before the lifetime of Padre Pérez, lends particular color to the legend.

In the years to come, the Franciscans of Guadalupe were often gratefully to recall the events of the fifteenth of August, 1844, and the predilection which Our Lady showed for them. The memory was a source of encouragement and consolation in the trials which the community was shortly to undergo.

---

*The explanation of how a ring could be placed on the finger of a painting of Our Lady, is this: the ring was made open, and the ends were pushed through holes in the canvas, and pressed flat on the reverse side of the painting.

In August of 1859, the religious were driven from their College of Guadalupe by the exclaustration laws, and took refuge in the Franciscan College of La Santa Cruz in Querétaro. In November of the same year they were forced to leave Querétaro, and went to the College of San Fernando, in Mexico. On Christmas Eve of 1850, the few Franciscans who remained at San Fernando had to don secular garb and sorrowfully take leave of the cloister.

Throughout all the trials and difficulties which the religious had to bear, Padre Pérez diligently fulfilled one responsible office after another in the dismembered community. Only in 1871, feeling the weight of his more than seventy years, was he able to relinquish the prelacy of the *Guadalupanos.* Then to prepare for his last journey, the venerable Franciscan retired to Tepotzotlán, some twenty-five miles north of Mexico City. He died there on the fifteenth of June, 1873.

The reader will recall Our Lady's promise to give the Guadalupe community "another ring" in return for theirs, to remind them of their contract with her. What was this second ring? And where is it today?

The constant and faithful companion of Padre Pérez in his retirement was a Franciscan Lay Brother, Salvador Carillo. When Brother Carillo died, he was buried in the same grave as his friend and spiritual father.

During the last illness of Padre Pérez, Brother Carillo and many other persons were watching in prayer by his bedside, in the home of the Pérez Tejada family. The watchers observed a very beautiful woman enter and approach the sickbed. She placed a ring upon the finger of the dying man. Later, Padre Pérez gave the ring to Brother Carillo, saying:

"Take it to your Mistress, who is the Immaculate Conception. It was she who brought it to me."

At that time the image of the Immaculate Conception was in the Pérez Tejada *casa* for nine days of prayer. Before Our Lady's likeness, as instructed, Brother Carillo deposited the ring. When the Brother died, in 1882, he left it to the Pérez Tejada family. From them it passed to a convent of nuns, *Las Monjas Sacramentarias del Espíritu Santo,* in San Angel, Mexico. They kept it in a reliquary on the Blessed Sacrament altar in their chapel.

The present writer had the good fortune to see and examine both rings. The ring of gold which Padre Pérez presented to the Blessed Virgin in 1844 is on the painting of Our Lady of Guadalupe in the chapel of the Franciscan Convent in Guadalupe, Zacatecas. The other ring, handed down by Padre Pérez to Brother Carillo, is now in the possession of a Franciscan formerly in the College of Guadalupe. It is made of human hair, delicately fashioned, and preserved in a small oval reliquary of silver.

Each year on the Feast of Our Lady's Assumption, the sons of Saint Francis in the Convent of Guadalupe carry out the devout practice introduced on the fifteenth of August, 1844, at Our Lady's command.

OUR LADY OF THE THUNDERBOLT
Guadalajara, Jalisco

XX

NUESTRA SEÑORA DEL RAYO

(OUR LADY OF THE THUNDERBOLT)

Guadalajara, Jalisco

*I*N THE first years of the nineteenth century, while Mexico enjoyed the double blessing of peace and religious liberty, a community of women was living out a tranquil, prayer-filled existence in Guadalajara. From 1699, when Bishop Felipe Galindo y Chávez had built them a dwelling in that city, next to the *ermita* of San Sebastián Martír, the Pious Sisterhood of Jesús Nazareño had lived and prayed there. In 1722, royal permission was received to found there a religious community of Dominicans. By 1768 they had constructed the temple which still exists today, the venerable Church of Jesús María. So far as history records, the quiet tenor of their sanctified life went on for many years unmarked by unusual incident. Then, in 1807, according to legend, an event occurred which was to change the life of the little community.

When the first seven Dominican nuns of the new foundation had arrived at their new community house in 1792, they found there an "image of the Most Holy Virgin, representing her glorious Assumption to the heavens." The nuns added a pearl rosary to the figure, converting it into an image of Our Lady of the Rosary. At first the statue was placed at the head of an ambulatory giving onto the gatekeeper's lodge. After

some years it ended up in a dormitory, neglected and virtually
forgotten by the nuns of Jesús María. Such was its situation
until August of the year 1807.

At two-thirty in the morning of the thirteenth of August,
a violent storm came up over Guadalajara. Rain rattled the
windows of the convent, and thunder caused its foundations
to quiver, while flashes of lightning made the cells brighter
than day. Suddenly a tremendous clap shook the dormitory
where some religious were asleep, and a bolt of lightning
hurled itself into the room extinguishing the solitary night
lamp. The dormitory filled with smoke, the acrid smell of
ozone mingled with the pungent fumes of charred wood and
burning fiber, while the darkness resounded with the screams
of frightened women. When the terrified nuns were able to
find and light a few candles, the uncertain flicker revealed a
sight that filled them with holy fear and wonder.

The statue of Our Lady stood in its accustomed place at
the head of the dormitory, between a painting of Saint Dominic and another canvas representing the Most Holy Trinity.
Neither painting had been damaged. A religious asleep on
a cot directly below the picture of Saint Dominic awoke
frightened but unharmed. The image of the Blessed Virgin
had not escaped, however. The thunderbolt had scorched its
vestments and the hair; the eyes, made of crystal, had been
shattered. At the same time, the Holy Child, resting upon the
arm of His Mother, was untouched. And wonderful to recount, the religious were all unhurt, although some of them
had been asleep within feet of the image.

To commemorate their remarkable escape, the community
carried the statue to the church adjoining their convent, and
a Mass of Thanksgiving was sung there the following day.
Upon its return to the convent, Our Lady's image was restored
to its place of honor in the convent chapel. There it remained,

an object of devout prayer and meditation. Then, five days later, there occurred the second in what was to prove a series of marvels connected with "Our Lady of the Thunderbolt" — *Nuestra Señora del Rayo* — as the image came to be called.

On the eighteenth of August in 1807, at three-thirty in the afternoon, two workmen accompanied Sor María Teresa de San Joaquín to the chapel. Under her direction, they were to carry the statue to the cell of a nun who was seriously ill. The chapel, illumined by the soft light of afternoon, suddenly darkened. A great thundercloud, a frequent phenomenon in Guadalajara during that season of rains, was passing across the sun. In the darkness of the chapel, the image of Our Lady suddenly took on an unearthly brightness. From head to breast it shone with a soft, intense glow. The astonished religious and the two *mozos* stood as if turned to stone. They were still in this attitude when the Prioress, Sor María Francesca de la Concepción, entered the choir with the other religious to sing Vespers. Sor María Teresa called out:

"Mother, see what the Most Holy Virgin is doing!"

There could be no doubt of this new happening. All the religious saw it. But for all their holy life, or, to be more accurate, *because* of it, nuns are among the world's most practical people. Thrilled as they were by this new sign of Mary's favor, they still, as religious, had a daily order of life to observe.

"Sisters," directed the Prioress, "we shall go on with Vespers."

And so, while a summer thunderstorm came up over Guadalajara, and the image of Our Lady radiated an unearthly light, the little community chanted the traditional Vesper Psalms. But the peace of the chapel did not last for long.

As the first notes of the Magnificat were intoned, a crash of thunder shook the chapel to its foundations. At the same moment, a flash of lightning half blinded the nuns by its brilliance. It was some minutes before they could observe what had happened.

The blackened features of Our Lady's image had resumed their rosy hue, though more beautiful, it seemed, than of old. Her eyes of crystal, burst and discolored the year before, now gazed clear and shining upon her dedicated daughters. The rosary at her girdle, formerly blackened and twisted, had regained its pearly luminosity.

These facts were verified by the chaplain of the Church of Jesús María, Don Manuel Cerviño (later Vicar Capitular of the cathedral), and by the Governor of the Episcopal Chancery, Don José María Gómez y Villaseñor (later Bishop-elect of Michoacán), who conducted the official investigation into the happenings.

Numerous are the verified favors and cures wrought through the gracious intercession of Our Lady of the Thunderbolt.

One of the very interesting narrations concerns a religious of the same convent, Sor María de Jesús Cecilia de San Cajetano, who was professed in 1839, at the age of nineteen. In 1842, Sor María fell ill of a fever which left her with spinal paralysis. For eight years she was attended by three of the most competent physicians of Guadalajara, who availed themselves of every aid the medical science of the day could offer. For a while their skill afforded her some relief. Occasionally, for instance, there would be a day when Sor María, with great pain and difficulty, could rise from her bed. Leaning on a stick and supported by another religious, she would attempt a few steps. But these attempts were painful in the extreme and finally had to be abandoned.

In August of 1850, Don Francisco Garibay, her personal physician, spoke to her:

"Sor María, there is no use in my coming to visit you any longer. I can do nothing to cure you — absolutely nothing."

"And the medicines, Doctor? Shall I keep on taking them?"

"I think not, Sor María. They can no longer help you."

But if medical science had despaired of helping the young religious, she herself did not lose hope. Night and day her prayers went heavenward to the throne of the Divine Physician, and to the feet of Mary, Health of the Sick.

Early one morning, the seventeenth of December of the same year, Sor María was seized with an overwhelming desire to visit the chapel of *Nuestra Señora del Rayo*. At nine-thirty in the morning she expressed this wish to the Subprioress, Sor María Joaquína.

"Madre, I should like you to take me to the chapel of Our Lady. If you will do this, I shall be so happy."

"Very well," replied the other religious. "Let us go, then."

And with the Subprioress' aid, Sor María slowly and painfully made her way to the chapel of Our Lady. But the journey had exhausted her completely, and she slumped to the floor at the feet of the sacred image. The Subprioress fetched her a pillow, saying:

"Now rest here and ask the Most Holy Virgin to let you walk again." And with that she left the chapel.

Alone at the feet of Our Lady's statue, Sor María Cecilia began to experience the first gnawings of despair. She later recounted that her soul had been sunk in the most sorrowful depression, not only then, but throughout the years of her illness. Her only consolation was "to place her afflicted heart in the hands of the Most Holy Virgin at the foot of the Cross."

"Oh, restore my health, Good Mother," she now prayed. "For if I continue like this, I fear for my salvation!"

Shortly after ten o'clock the Subprioress re-entered the chapel with two religious, and they prayed for a few minutes with Sor María. At eleven-fifteen two other nuns came to ask Sor María whether they might help her back to her cell before the noonday meal.

"Let me see whether I can manage alone," she replied.

Unaided, she got to her feet and slowly walked to her cell, where she sat down. The two nuns, who had followed her, looked at her in astonishment. Gone was the pain from her face, replaced by a joyful radiance that betokened inner health.

About noon, when one of the nuns brought her meal, Sor María was walking back and forth in her cell. Seeing the other religious, she smiled happily and cried:

"Sister, tell the other nuns to come and see me walking!"

In a few minutes the entire community had gathered at the door of her cell.

"Watch me, Sisters! Who would ever believe that it is I?" cried Sor María. And before the gaze of the amazed religious, she walked rapidly from her cell, down the corridor and back, into her cell and out again. Her face shone with health; her eyes glowed with delight.

"I can't believe it's I! I must be someone else!"

Directing her steps toward the chapel, she prostrated herself before Our Lady's image. The community, which had followed her to the chapel, chanted a Magnificat in thanksgiving to Our Lady. Then, for the first time in many years, Sor María mounted the steps to the choir, in her eagerness taking them two at a time.

By now it was one-thirty, and the Subprioress ordered Sor María to take her luncheon. The narrative, full of charming little incidents showing the human side of religious life, relates that after luncheon Sor María went walking up and down the steps, delightedly enjoying her newly recovered health.

Sor María lived almost twenty years longer, and until her death on the fourth of March in 1870, enjoyed perfect health. This is affirmed by the records kept in the Convent of Jesús María.

Another notable cure attributed to the intercession of *Nuestra Señora del Rayo* is that of Doña Micaela Gómez de Contreras, stricken with spinal paralysis in 1824. She was completely and instantly cured on the seventeenth of September, 1856, while the image of Our Lady was being carried from the Convent to the Church of Jesús María for the celebration of a Solemn Mass in her honor.

The Pontifical Coronation of *Nuestra Señora del Rayo* took place in the cathedral of Guadalajara on the eighteenth of August, 1940. On this occasion the sixth Archbishop of Guadalajara, Don José Garibi Rivera, acted as Pontifical Delegate of His Holiness, placing a crown of gold upon the sacred image.

The statue of *Nuestra Señora del Rayo* is forty-one inches in height. Its features are majestic, though somewhat severe; the coloring is a delicate pink, and the eyes have a slight downward cast. On her left arm the Virgin holds the Infant Jesus, and in her right hand there are a rosary and a golden scepter. The images are richly vested in ornately embroidered robes. Our Lady wears golden earrings and a necklace of pearls. Behind her head is an aureole of finely chased and gilded silver. At her feet is a half-moon of silver, upheld by two cherubim. The whole is supported upon a pedestal of deeply chased silver. The crowns of gold worn by Mother and Child, as well as their scepters, are studded with pearls and precious stones.

The eighteenth of August each year, anniversary of the statue's miraculous restoration, is the principal feast of *Nuestra Señora del Rayo.* This celebration is inaugurated by a Solemn Novena of Masses and devotions. At this time devout worshipers come from all over Guadalajara and from other parts of Jalisco, to the Church of Jesús María. At two o'clock in the afternoon of the eighteenth of August, the bells of Jesús María ring out, and thousands of voices are raised in the solemn *Te Deum,* giving thanks to God for the wonders He has wrought through the image of Our Lady.

OUR LADY OF OCOTLÁN
Tlaxcala, Tlaxcala

XXI

NUESTRA SEÑORA DE OCOTLAN

(OUR LADY OF OCOTLÁN)

Tlaxcala, Tlaxcala

IN PRE-HISPANIC times, Tlaxcala was basically a warrior state, like Sparta, and equally indomitable. The Moctezumas could never subdue it, and Hernán Cortés succeeded in making an ally of it only by treaty, at a critical moment in his enterprise.

Not only were the people of Tlaxcala the first friends of Cortés in the New World; they were also the first to become Christians. In the Convent of San Francisco, the oldest in New Spain, there is a chapel of the same name in which can be seen the pulpit where the Gospel was preached for the first time, and the font where the four "senators" of Tlaxcala were baptized, with Cortés himself as their godfather. The convent is of characteristic sixteenth-century construction. Especially worthy of attention are its superb arches, and the majestic separate tower, the only one of its kind in the country. The façade is simple and severe, and the interior has one nave of regular proportions. The altars are pure Churrigueresque; the roof is of cedar painted in blue with gilt stars, and with a richly decorated ceiling. This convent is closely connected with our story.

135

Other buildings in Tlaxcala also go back to the colonial epoch. The governor's palace, for example, while it has undergone some changes, still retains much of its original fortress-like aspect. Its reception hall is soberly elegant, and contains an unusual set of handsomely embroidered chairs. The municipal palace is of the same period and has preserved the decorative motifs of sixteenth-century Mexican architecture.

Undoubtedly, however, the most interesting single edifice in this city of legend is the sanctuary of the Holy Virgin of Ocotlán, on a hill outside the city walls. Its façade and towers are Churrigueresque. Within, the profuseness of gold, on altars and images, literally dazzles the eye. There are more than two hundred pieces of sculpture. The image of the Virgin of Ocotlán stands high above and behind the main altar of the church. It is her story that we now have to tell.

In the early months of the year 1541, the territory of Tlaxcala was stricken with a plague of smallpox, which swept through the countryside like a tidal wave, leaving hardly a family untouched. It is estimated that nine out of ten Indians within the area died within a short time. To make matters worse, the native *curanderos* (medicine men) had no experience with the disease, and were unable to take or suggest countermeasures. The burning fever which the plague brought on drove the people to the rivers to bathe; they believed, in their simplicity, that the waters would cure or lessen their sickness. The water of one stream, the Zahuapan, was especially valued, as it was believed to possess medicinal properties for diseases of the skin.

Among the families stricken by the pestilence was that of Juan Diego, who worked for the *frailes* of the Franciscan convent in Tlaxcala. Juan Diego obtained permission to go to the Rio Zahuapan and draw some of the healing waters for his stricken relatives in Xiloxostla. Accordingly he took a water jar, and walked down the mountain from the convent, filled his jar, and continued on toward Xiloxostla in the waning light of the early spring afternoon. Crossing the western slope of the Cerro de San Lorenzo, he began to make his way through a dense grove of ocote, a tree indigenous to the region. Of a sudden, Juan Diego found his pathway blocked by a very beautiful woman of regal mien. She greeted him in a gracious fashion: "May God preserve you, my son! Where are you bound for?"

The humble Indian, taken by surprise, could not find speech for several moments, but the amiable regard of the lady reassured him, and he replied: "I am taking some water from the *rio* to my sick ones, who are dying."

"Then follow me," said the lady. "I will give you water to cure the disease. It will cure, not only your family, but all who drink of it. My heart is every ready to help those who are ill, for I cannot bear to see their misfortune."

At the words of the mysterious lady, it was as though a great weight had been lifted from the shoulders of Juan Diego. True, in all his travels through the ocote grove he had never seen a spring of water there, yet he obediently followed his new acquaintance with a light step and a lighter heart. When they had come to a slight break in the rise, at a point where the path approached a barranca, the new-found benefactress indicated a lively spring of clear water.

"Take as much as you wish of this water," she said. "And know that those who are touched by even the tiniest drop will obtain, not merely relief from their illness, but perfect health."

Juan Diego obediently emptied his water jar, and refilled it from the marvelous spring. He was now anxious to be on his way to Xiloxostla, and turned to beg leave to depart. But the lady stayed him with a gesture. There was a message for him to carry to the Franciscans at San Lorenzo.

"Tell the religious for me that in this place they will find my image. It will not only manifest my perfections, but through it I shall generously bestow favors and kindnesses. When they find the image, they are to place it in the chapel of San Lorenzo."

With the words of his beautiful benefactress ringing in his ears, Juan Diego continued on his way to Xiloxostla. The jar of water, which before had pressed so heavily on his shoulder, now seemed almost weightless, as, joyous and confident, he ran the rest of the way to his pueblo. Greeting his afflicted ones, he lovingly offered them the health-giving water. As the legend relates, no sooner had they drunk of the water than their sickness departed, leaving them whole and sound.

Filled with joy at their unexpected fortune, Juan Diego and his family hurried out into the pueblo to make known the good news to their friends and neighbors. Good tidings travel quickly, and in minutes the narrow little street was filled with Indians, eager to crowd into the tiny house and hear the tale from the lips of Juan Diego himself. Time and again Juan had to relate the apparition of *Zoapiltzin* ("The Lady Woman") who had directed him to the miraculous spring. And, equally important, he had to share with his townsfolk the miraculous water, for there was scarcely a dwelling that did not house the desperately sick. Juan had to dole out the precious liquid carefully, but everyone who had a sick parent, spouse, or child, received a few drops. And, true to the promise of *Zoapiltzin,* all who imbibed the water recovered instant health, so that shortly the plague had disappeared from Xiloxostla.

By this time night had fallen upon the pueblo, so Juan Diego was unable to return to San Lorenzo. But with the first streaks of dawn in the sky, the Indian was on the road to the convent. There he lost no time in recounting to the *frailes* his marvelous adventures of the day before, including the message which the beautiful *Zoapiltzin* had given him for them. Needless to say, the religious listened carefully to the narrative; but, prudent men that they were, they reserved judgment upon it. Juan Diego was told that they would investigate the matter, and sent about his ordinary tasks. Later in the day they requestioned him very carefully, to determine whether they might find some inconsistency in his recital. The Indian, however, with the utmost simplicity, merely reaffirmed, time and again, what he had said the first time. Still later in the afternoon, a third interrogation merely repeated the original tale.

The consistency of the *criado's* story under the most searching cross-examination could not fail to impress the Franciscans. They convened a special chapter to deliberate the matter. Finally they decided to see for themselves the place of the alleged apparition and miraculous spring. They would wait until the natives in the vicinity of the convent had retired for the night, and then send Juan Diego to the spring for water, following him unobserved.

Juan Diego was instructed accordingly; and he left the monastery confines, closely followed by a number of the religious moving as noiselessly as possible, so as not to awaken the villagers. Nevertheless, their departure was noted by more than one of the natives, with much curiosity and possibly with not a little alarm. Were the *padres* going to leave them? If not, why were they moving so stealthily and at such an unaccustomed hour? No one ever traveled in Tlaxcala at night except in a grave emergency. The strange happening passed from mouth to mouth, and from house to house, and in a short time the *frailes* found themselves accompanied by a goodly number of villagers, determined to see the matter to its conclusion.

At last the strangely assorted group rounded the eastern slope of the Cerro de San Lorenzo and reached the ocote grove. What a sight met their eyes! The grove was afire. One great tree in particular seemed to be burning along its entire length, its branches glowing redly against the night. The enormous size of the tree and the fact that apparently it alone, although the largest of the trees, had been entirely ablaze, aroused the wonder of both *padres* and natives. But it was now very late at night, and no more could be done until daylight. So, marking the location of the great ocote carefully, the Franciscans returned to the convent.

Shortly after the community Mass had been offered the next morning, the missioners, accompanied now by a considerable number of the Tlaxcaltecans, once again directed their steps to the scene of the previous night's happenings. Upon arrival, they noted that the fire had extinguished itself, the damage being mainly confined to the smaller branches of the trees. That in itself was occasion for surprise, because it was still the dry season, and ordinarily the ocote, once ignited — it is a torch pine of extremely resinous character — will burn up completely. Equally strangely, the great ocote, which they had carefully marked the night before, had been consumed much more than its lesser fellows, which is contrary to the usual circumstance of such fires.

On the orders of the Guardian, one of the community had brought an ax. He was instructed to chop down the trunk of the large tree, which after some time he succeeded in doing. At this point let us refer to an earlier Mexican chronicler:

"A new marvel met their eyes: within the trunk of the fallen tree was visible the image of the Holy Mother of God, representing the mystery of her Immaculate Conception — which can be seen today in the temple lovingly erected later by her children. . . . In this manner the tale of Juan Diego was fully verified, in the presence of many witnesses. The apparition of the Virgin Mary to her servant Juan Diego was a happy reality, on the day she showed him the medicinal water and sent him to advise the religious where they would find her sacred image."

Fulfilling what was, to his mind, evidently a command from heaven, the Guardian had the image carried in procession to the chapel of San Lorenzo. To calm the excited Indians and give a semblance of order to the procedure, he ordered them to cut off branches of ocote and walk in files, singing their simple hymns and reciting various prayers and litanies. Behind them came the *frailes,* to several of whom had been entrusted the actual bearing of the ocote image. When they arrived at the chapel, the Guardian had the statue placed in the niche of the titular patron, San Lorenzo, whose figure was removed for that purpose. The entire pueblo joined with the religious in a service of thanksgiving for the special grace that had been vouchsafed them all.

But every community must be allowed a "doubting Thomas," and it appears that there was one at San Lorenzo. The Indian sacristan of the chapel took it very ill that his patron, San Lorenzo, had been forced to make way for a new favorite. He waited until nightfall, and after everyone had retired, he entered the church and took down the image of the Virgin, restoring San Lorenzo to his accustomed place. Then, satisfied at having served his patron well, the good man relocked the chapel and went home to the sleep of the just. The following morning, to his dismay, the Virgin was back in the principal niche, and San Lorenzo was again relegated to one side. Thinking that someone hiding in the chapel the night before had rearranged the statues, he determined to out-smart the culprit. That night he once again restored San

Lorenzo to the main altar, with the added precaution that this time he took the image of the Virgin to his own house.

All in vain; the following morning, upon unlocking the chapel, he saw Our Lady's image once more above the altar, with San Lorenzo upon a side table. But, with the stubbornness characteristic of his race, the luckless fellow would not give up. That night, for the third time he replaced San Lorenzo in the main niche. To make doubly sure that no one would trick him, the sacristan put the image of Our Lady in a large case used for storing the ornaments of the chapel. This he closed, spreading his serape over it. Then he lay down to sleep. Upon arising the next morning, he found the case empty, and the Virgin's image again above the altar. Finally convinced of the supernatural character of the events, and almost frightened out of his wits, the Indian rushed to explain to the religious what he had done, dreading not so much the chastisement he might receive from them as the heavenly wrath he feared he had called down upon himself.

From that time down to the present day, the image of Our Lady has been venerated in Tlaxcala. From earliest times it was called *Nuestra Señora de Ocotlatía,* that is "Our Lady of the Burning Ocote," which has come down to us as "Our Lady of Ocotlán." The present-day name, which refers to the "place of the ocote," is a perpetual reminder of the apparition, of the fire, and of the wood from which the image is formed.

The figure of Our Lady of Ocotlán appears to be carved, and of one piece. Its height is a little more than fifty-eight inches. The body is gently inclined forward. The features are those of a young woman; the eyes are painted, and the brows gently arched; the mouth is small and delicately formed, and the nose straight and somewhat narrow. The well-formed hands are joined in the traditional attitude of prayer. Unfortunately, in contravention of the Church's prohibition against the retouching of images of great fame and antiquity, the venerable statue has often suffered restorative measures by hands somewhat less than competent.

The present vestments, changed according to the various feasts, cover the original carven foot-length tunic and the gilt-ornamented mantle, passing over the left shoulder and beneath the right arm and gathered into a cincture at the waist. The head and the golden imperial crown surmounting it are surrounded by an aureole with a dozen stars. The image stands upon a pedestal of silver, a crescent moon, associated throughout Mexico with representations of the Immaculate Conception, at its feet.

The sanctuary of Ocotlán was in the care of the Franciscans for ninety-nine years, from 1541 to 1640. This fact is commemorated in the Churrigueresque façade of the present-day church, with the likeness of Saint Francis sculptured above the entrance.

In 1746, the sanctuary of Our Lady of Ocotlán was aggregated to the Liberian Basilica of Saint Mary Major in Rome, where is kept a sacred image of Our Lady thought by some to have been painted by Saint Luke the Evangelist. At the same time, devout visitors to the sanctuary of Our Lady of Ocotlán were granted the Indulgences, privileges, and Apostolic Indults which might be gained by personally visiting the Roman Basilica itself. In 1755, Our Lady of Ocotlán was named Patroness of the Province of Tlaxcala (now Puebla). An Apostolic Brief of Pope Clement XIII in 1766 conceded the faculty of celebrating the Feast of the Patronage annually on a Sunday in July. The apparition of Our Lady of Ocotlán to Juan Diego is celebrated on Quinquagesima Sunday, falling usually in the month of February. In commemoration of the finding of the image, the people of Ocotlán walk in procession carrying branches of ocote and flowers plucked along the way-

side. In 1906, the Holy See granted to the sanctuary of
Ocotlán the status of a collegiate church, with its chapter of
canons, and gave permission for the liturgical coronation of
the image of Our Lady of Ocotlán.

The present-day pilgrim will find the journey, whether
from Mexico City or from Puebla, picturesque and memorable.
In the sleepy little village of Ocotlán the clock will turn back
for him more than four hundred years, which number just
about equals the present population of the hamlet. After
visiting Our Lady's shrine, one should pay a visit to *La Capilla
del Pocito* — the chapel which stands in the ancient grove
where Our Lady appeared, and the spot whence sprang the
health-giving water. One may also visit Xiloxostla, the birth-
place of Juan Diego, and the *Oratorio de Juan Diego,* now the
sacristy of the *Templo de Santa Isabel.* His earthly remains
are believed to be interred alongside the altar in the oratory.
His soul, we trust, is enjoying the happiness of the blessed
in the presence of his beloved *Zoapiltzin.*

OUR LADY OF TONATICO
Tonatico, Mexico

NUESTRA SEÑORA DE FONATICO, MEX.

XXII

LA SANTISIMA VIRGEN DE TONATICO

(OUR LADY OF TONATICO)

Tonatico, Mexico

ONATICO is a little village near the internationally known spa of Ixtapan de la Sal, in the state of Mexico. The tourist and vacationer in search of recreation and rest, and the invalid in quest of health, speed along the highway on their way to the health-giving waters of Ixtapan de la Sal, with never a thought given to the insignificant little pueblo they are passing through. Yet to the simple inhabitants of Tonatico and the surrounding countryside, their pueblo contains a treasure far and away more precious than the justly vaunted springs of their wealthier neighbor. Their pious legends concerning an image of Our Lady in the sanctuary of Tonatico have brought thousands to the feet of this statue in the past two hundred years.

Upon the completion of the sanctuary in Tonatico, so an early legend relates, the *padre* in charge of the parish invited the priests from the surrounding village parishes to assist him in celebrating the blessing of his new church. During the banquet and the festivities which followed the solemnities, two of the invited guests were relating to the pastor a curious dream, which, by strange coincidence, they both had experienced a short time before. The purport of the dream was that

145

this work of building a church was to cause the pastor a great deal of toil and anxiety. The company was discussing the unusual circumstance when a parishioner came running in with an alarming message: the church was on fire! Pastor and guests rushed out in dismay to the scene of the catastrophe — too late to do anything but look on in consternation while the flames mounted higher and higher. At last the roof crashed in, a mass of burning timbers.

There was only one consoling feature to the tragedy. In some unexplained manner, the statue of Our Lady had escaped damage. Stranger yet, the image was found outside the church, looking upward, as if watching the destruction of her temple. The head of the statue still appears today as tilted at a curious angle. One explanation given is that the heat of the flames had caused the change in attitude; yet the fire had not otherwise damaged it. All the parishioners solemnly denied having removed the statue from the burning church, and the mystery remains unsolved to this day.

From that time, the devotion of the people increased, and through the years they have appealed to Our Lady of Tonatico for help in their spiritual and temporal necessities. Ex-votos and testimonials by the hundreds give evidence today of the faith and devotion which this image has inspired. The people of Tonatico will relate to you any number of favors which Our Blessed Lady has visited upon them. Some of the better known legends are recounted here.

In the year 1780, a certain Don José María, who was stricken with a grave illness, sought out the most able physicians in the countryside. The medical men put all their skill and experience into the effort to save him. Finally, however, they declared the case beyond hope, and agreed that the old gentleman had at best a few days of life remaining. Shortly afterward the physicians' prognostication came true: Don José

died. It frequently happens in serious trouble that even the
least religious families bethink themselves of God. The relatives of Don José went to the sanctuary of Our Lady of
Tonatico. They besought her to lay her hand upon his head
and restore him to life. God heard the prayer of His holy
Mother — Don José returned to life. Not only that, but like
the son of the widow of Naim, he sat up whole and sound,
giving not the least indication that he had ever been ill.
Accompanied by his grateful family, Don José went to the
shrine of Our Lady of Tonatico, where they dedicated a plaque
commemorating his marvelous restoration to life and health.

The story of Don Manuel Zariñana is another favorite
with the *Tonaticenses*. One day in the year 1783, Don Manuel
was in the fields with his *peónes,* overseeing the loading of
grain into a wagon. Suddenly, from the darkening sky that
betokened a summer rainstorm, a bolt of lightning darted
earthward, leaving one of the workmen apparently dead and
the others stunned. The noise of the thunderclap brought
Don Manuel's household running into the field. They arrived
in time to see the landowner and his workers slowly recovering
consciousness. The newcomers at once applied their rough
first aid, and soon all the victims were on their feet, still dazed
but otherwise unharmed — all, that is, but one. This poor
fellow did not respond to the most heroic efforts to revive
him, and eventually he was given up for dead.

Some members of the household stood around bemoaning
the tragedy. Others acted in a way that does credit to their
presence of mind as well as to their faith. They ran to the
pueblo, to the sanctuary of Our Lady of Tonatico, relating
what had happened and begging permission to take the precious image back with them. The request was granted, and
reverent hands bore the statue back to the field, and placed it

upon the body of the victim, with prayers and entreaties to
the Virgin.

Our Lady heard their request. While they were praying,
the inanimate figure was seen to move, and finally the laborer
recovered consciousness, none the worse for his terrifying experience. In gratitude the man repaired to the sanctuary with
his companions, where ultimately a plaque was dedicated in
thanksgiving.

That Our Lady of Tonatico has a special predilection for
the children under her care is demonstrated by the following
account:

In July, 1892, a small child named José Albarrán was play-
ing about the patio of his home in Terrero. Venturing too
near the well, he fell in. When evening came on and the child
was not to be found, his mother, Juana Estrada de Albarrán,
went looking for him, but to no avail. She called on her
neighbors for help, and they searched the surrounding countryside without finding the youngster. When it was almost dark,
the child's older sister, Julia, went to the well for water, and
espied the hand of her brother sticking out of the water.
Drawn by the cries of the girl, the rest of the family came
upon the scene, and at length after some difficulty, succeeded
in drawing the little body from the water. The child appeared
dead.

The sorrowing family laid the boy upon a couch, and someone went to fetch an image of Our Lady of Tonatico which
was in the house. They placed the sacred statue upon the
head of the child, and all fell upon their knees, beseeching
Our Lady to restore the life of little José. For hours they
knelt, their prayers going heavenward to the throne of the
Queen of Grace. About three o'clock in the morning, the child
suddenly sat up, saying that he was hungry and wanted something to eat. He was completely himself; more, he never after-

ward experienced the slightest ill effect from his accident. The rejoicing family dedicated a *retablo* in the sanctuary of Our Lady of Tonatico as a perpetual testimonial of gratitude for the boy's miraculous restoration.

A less dramatic but nonetheless impressive intervention was attributed to Our Lady of Tonatico by one Don José Hernández. In January of the year 1890, Hernández suffered an infection of the eyes, and began doctoring himself, as the country folk are wont to do, with household remedies. The disease only became worse, and he finally betook himself to one physician, and then another. Their prescribed medicines had no effect, and at last he could not use his eyes at all. What was even harder to bear, the physicians told him that there was no known remedy for the condition.

At this juncture Don José threw himself upon the help of heaven, begging the Most Holy Virgin of Tonatico to aid him. Toward the end of January, the infection had reached such a point that everyone believed he would never see again. But the afflicted man continued to implore Our Lady's help. And then, all in a moment, Don José Hernández recovered the use of his eyes completely, without the use of medicines. The infection disappeared and his sight was perfectly restored. This cure was commemorated by an ex-voto placed by the grateful beneficiary at the shrine of Our Lady of Tonatico.

A more recent *retablo* at the shrine, this one of the year 1918, commemorates a remarkable escape from death. On the eighteenth of August in that year, Petronillo Román and his wife, on horseback, were riding along the edge of the steep barranca of Manilaltenango. As the mount of the woman would not quicken its pace, Petronillo foolishly gave it a blow with his whip. The startled horse reared violently, throwing its rider out over the barranca. As she felt herself falling, she invoked the help of Our Lady of Tonatico. Her fall was

arrested by the branches of a tree growing out between the
rocks on the downward slope. She was uninjured — but sus-
pended in midair, between earth and sky. What was to be
done? It seemed impossible that she could be rescued without
ropes, and at any moment the branch which supported her
might give way, letting her fall to death on the rocks below.
Again the woman recommended herself to the care of Our
Lady of Tonatico, calling upon the Holy Virgin to deliver her
from this danger. In a moment, as the testimonial relates, she
found herself once more beside her husband at the top of the
barranca, unhurt and able to continue the journey. While the
retablo is not clear on the exact manner in which the Señora
de Román was rescued, the faith and devotion of Don Petronillo and his wife are evident in their testimonial.

There is a favorite prayer of the people of Tonatico when
they invoke Our Lady. It tells her that they consider her, as it
were, the Pole Star at the zenith of their little world, enlight-
ening and guiding their souls by her brilliant rays. We may
be sure that the firm and simple faith which directs such a
prayer will not go unrewarded.

OUR LADY OF IZAMAL
Izamal, Yucatán

XXII

NUESTRA SEÑORA DE IZAMAL

(OUR LADY OF IZAMAL)

Izamal, Yucatán

*H*ISTORIC and fabulous Yucatán — land of the Maya, that mysterious and highly civilized race, which in many ways had far outstripped in progress the civilization of Europe at the time when the Spaniards were beginning their conquest of Mexico. Village and settlement off the beaten track are the dwelling places of those descended from that proud race, speaking the same language, maintaining the customs and arts of their ancestors. The present-day traveler in Yucatán visits the remains of their marvelous cities, once centers of a pagan religion and culture — Kabah, Latna, Chichén Itzá, Uxmal — and present-day Mérida, the capital, built on the site of the famed Tiho of pre-Cortesian times.

The Mayan worshiped a spirit god, Hunabku, as the Franciscan missionaries found, and used a cross to represent the "tree of life." They practiced a form of baptism, believing that thus their children would be "born again," and they upheld the sanctity of the marriage bond. It was not strange, then, that the Yucatecan should have been drawn by his religious nature to the *cultus* and love of Mary Immaculate. When Cortés landed on Cozumel in March of 1519, among his first acts was to erect an image of the Most Pure Virgin

151

Mary. Diego de Landa relates that the first Spanish words the Mayan pronounced were:

"María! María! Cortés, Cortés!"

Upon the site of one of their ancient and picturesque communities the Spaniards built a city, Izamal. Its church and convent stand upon the platform of a great Mayan pyramid. It is in this church that the image of Our Lady of Izamal is enshrined.

As Izamal was the center and headquarters for the Mayan priesthood, the missionaries especially dedicated that area to the Virgin Mary. One of the three communities they erected was that of San Antonio de Izamal. When they first came to the region, the Franciscans lodged in the dwellings built by the earlier Mayas for the priests of their idols. We are indebted for a description of the city at this period to Juan de la Cueva Santillán, the Conquistador who was the *encomendero* of Izamal. Writing in the year 1581, he relates:

"The site of Izamal was an ancient settlement, with many large buildings of stonemasonry, vaulted and mortared. The monastery was established in the chief of these, which had leading up to it a stairway of more than a hundred and fifty steps, each more than half a *vara* high. The building faced north, and was surmounted by three great wall towers of considerable height. The largest of these towers faced the south, and the lesser ones faced east and west. Upon these towers were mortar figures which looked like giants armed with buckler and helmet. The natives say that their builders were of greater stature than the present-day people. The inhabitants of Izamal were conquered by Kakupacat and Vilo, courageous *capitanes* of the Itzáes who dwelt in Mayapán. The first inhabitants were called *Kinich-kabul, Kinich-kakmo, Quitahcutz, Quitahcoy,* from whom descend the *Joles, Moes* and *Coyes,* Indian names in this province."

Fray Antonio de Ciudad Real, writing in 1588, adds to our knowledge:

"The convent of Izamal, named for Saint Anthony, is completed, with upper and lower cloister, sleeping quarters and church, all constructed of stonemasonry and vaulting, built upon a great mound, with many steps leading up to it. The mound was leveled somewhat in order to build it, after the razing of a proud and ancient building of masonry, with stones of unusual size, as long as they were wide, placed one above the other and exceedingly well finished. Before the convent was built, the *frailes* occupied this building for a long time, as it contained apartments for cells and for religious functions, all quite ample. A very old and trustworthy *fraile* used to affirm that when the building was razed, such a great number of bats flew out that they destroyed a cattle ranch where they finally settled."

Fray Diego de Landa was named Guardian of the convent of Izamal in 1553. He it was who tore down a temple to the god Humpictok, and other buildings on the summit of Ppappholchac, and on the site began the convent and a church dedicated to the Immaculate Conception. The church was completed in 1554 and the convent in 1561.

When he arrived in Yucatán, Padre Landa enthusiastically set about learning the Mayan tongue. In a short while he had surpassed his teacher, Fray Luis de Villapando, and emended the latter's Mayan grammar. Once expert in the language, he obtained permission to go into the interior, cross in hand, converting the Indians. For this reason the natives used to call him "the missionary of the Cross."

A man of tremendous energy, Fray Diego fired the enthusiasm of the natives for the construction project at Izamal. They were proud and happy to work side by side with this

padre, who with his own hands cut down trees and hauled
stone for the buildings.

In order to draw the Indians more closely to the true religion, Padre de Landa journeyed in 1558 to Guatemala, the
great New World center of religious art, to procure an image
of the Blessed Virgin. He arranged at the same time to pur-
chase another for the convent in Mérida. In the *coro* of the
church in Guatemala was a statue of Our Lady the report of
whose beauty had reached the Franciscans at Yucatán through
a sketch brought thither, probably by one of the friars. Upon
his arrival in Guatemala, Padre de Landa inquired for its sculptor and found him still living, though advanced in years —
a Franciscan lay brother, Fray Juan de Aguirre. Padre de
Landa entreated him to make an image just like the original
for the church at Izamal, and another for the Franciscan convent in Mérida. Fray Juan undertook the charge at once, and
in a short while the two images were completed.

On the return journey, so the tradition relates, Our Lady
began to manifest for her children of Yucatán the special
predilection with which she has favored them to this day.
To make transportation easier along the two hundred leagues
of primitive and rugged roads between Guatemala and Yucatán, both statues were enclosed in one case, which was borne
on the shoulders of Fray Diego's Indian companions. It was
observed that, although the rains were frequent and heavy,
the area about the bearers and their cargo always remained
dry. Naturally there was great competition among the Indians
to carry the case.

The story continues. When the party came to Valladolid,
some Spaniards there, struck by the beauty of the statue, tried
to retain it for their convent, saying it was too fine to be
hidden away in an Indian pueblo. Of course Fray Diego and
his flock protested, but their words carried little weight with

the Spaniards. At this critical point Our Lady showed clearly whose side she took in the affair. When the citizens of Valladolid attempted to take the image by force, all their combined strength was unequal to the task of budging it from the ground an inch. Finally they had to give in and allow the *fraile* and his flock to continue on to Izamal.

Great was the admiration and gratitude of the Izamal folk when they learned of these marks of Mary's predilection for them. An early historian of Our Lady of Izamal, Padre Lizana, gives us a graphic picture of the devotion which she inspired from the beginning:

"Although she is visited throughout the year, it is principally on her feast, the eighth of December, day of her Immaculate Conception, that there is an almost innumerable gathering of Spaniards, mestizos, mulattos, Negroes, and Indians from all this country, as far as Cozumel, Tabasco, and even Chiapas. Every year it is celebrated with the greatest *fiestas* possible here. On those days the roads are so crowded with Indians from every quarter that they appear like swarms of ants. Many Spaniards of both sexes, from the time they espy her holy temple afar off in the distance, approach it on foot. But what causes the most devotion is to see the veneration with which the Indians approach it. As has already been said, the temple is on a hill, with numerous steps leading up to it. There are many who go on their knees the whole distance from the bottom, through the patio and the church, until they arrive at the base of the altar, which is placed in the center of the chapel for the *fiesta*. There they offer the gifts which, according to their little means, they bring. After kissing the hem of the frontal they return, greatly consoled, to their homes."

The original image is described as being of wood, sculptured its entire length and *estofada,* that is, polychromed over gilt. Its height is given in the earliest chronicle as *"cinco cuartas y seis dedos,"* which would have been slightly more than forty-six inches. The features are majestic and grave, of a light and somewhat pale color, and the hands joined before the breast. In former times the image was adorned with many jewels donated by the inhabitants of Mérida in gratitude for relief from a plague. The image had a throne of hammered silver, curiously wrought and of great value, and the litter upon which it was carried in procession was covered with silver. Many silver lamps hung before its altar, and the number of ex-votos and *milagros* on the walls grew so great that many of them had to be removed to make way for newer ones.

Perhaps the devotion of the people of Izamal, and of the Yucatecans generally, to Our Lady of Izamal is never so evident as in times of crisis, but even then it is only a more intense manifestation of the deep and abiding faith so characteristic of the Mexican people. One or two examples from history will bear out the strength and deeply rooted nature of that faith.

In August, 1648, a great epidemic raged across the peninsula of Yucatán. In this necessity, the people turned to Our Lady of Izamal, solemnly and publicly consecrating the province to her as their special patroness "against epidemics, illness, and public calamities." They promised to celebrate the Feast of the Assumption every year as an official public act of government. That the plague abated quickly and disappeared, was attributed to the direct intercession of Our Lady.

Toward the end of the seventeenth century Yucatán experienced a recurrence of the plague, which, together with the depredations of pirates on Spanish shipping and the sacking of coastal towns, led the Spanish government to fear that their entire colonial enterprise might be wiped out. In the

Villa of Campeche the plague raged so fiercely that it was feared that the town would have to be abandoned. Those who fled into Mérida probably took the infection with them, for within a month the capital was one vast hospital of dead and dying. In this extremity, the *Cabildo* at Mérida begged the Provincial of the Franciscans to bring Our Lady of Izamal to the capital for a solemn novena of prayer. The Provincial, Fray Bernardo de Sosa, agreed, and as he would entrust the image to the charge of no one else, made arrangements to journey to Izamal in person.

When the Indians in the towns along the coast heard that it was planned to take Our Lady to Mérida, they thronged into Izamal in order to accompany her. On the other hand, the inhabitants of Izamal were deeply disturbed, fearing that the image, once taken to Mérida, would never be returned to them. So they refused to allow the Provincial to touch it, declaring that they would protect it if necessary, by hiding it in the mountains. Fray Bernardo tried to calm them with the assurance that the city of Mérida and the *Cabildo* would vouch for its safe return. The Indians then presented a curious document to Fray Bernardo, in the name of the officials of all the pueblos of the region. It gave him custody of the image for seventeen days only, allowing nine days in Mérida for the novena and eight days for the journey to and from the capital. In this document Fray Bernardo was held personally responsible for the safekeeping and return of Our Lady of Izamal. He was asked to sign it; and sign it he did. Even at that, many of the Indians from Izamal went along on the journey to keep an eye on their beloved *Señora!*

Along with these public and general testimonials of faith and confidence in Our Lady on the part of the people of Yucatán, there merits to be recorded the devotion of many individuals. One of these was Don Antonio de Figueroa y

Silva, Brigadier and Field Marshal. In the year 1730 he was Governor of Yucatán. To this day he remains one of the finest examples of a class of men sent by Spain to the New World to direct the destinies of her people. Progressive and enterprising, he built a fine system of public roads, recolonized the Villa of Bacalar with families brought from the Canary Islands, and drove the British out of the Spanish territory of Belize. He beautified and modernized the cities of Campeche and Mérida, building new streets and temples in both places.

In that same year of 1730 the plague had stricken Mérida, and as we have seen above, Our Lady of Izamal was carried to the cathedral in the capital for a novena of prayer. Governor Figueroa came to the cathedral, and kneeling before the sacred image, placed at her feet the golden staff of the governor's office. By this act he signalized the profound gratitude of the entire people of Yucatán to Mary for having abated the plague which had been afflicting them for so long. In this way, too, the Governor publicly acclaimed Our Lady of Izamal the Patroness and real Governor, the *Capitana General,* of Yucatán. Afterward, dressed in the simple garments of a penitent, the Governor accompanied Our Lady for the four days of her return journey to Izamal. What a shining example this most Catholic knight and gentleman has set for those whose duty it is to rule over states and nations!

In 1829, the seventeenth of April was Thursday of Holy Week, and the altar and shrine of the sanctuary at Izamal was a blaze of light from hundreds of candles. By some misfortune the furnishings of the altar caught fire, and the resulting conflagration left the image of Our Lady in ashes. But consolation was to come from a most unexpected quarter, an example of the way in which Our Lady turns evil into good.

At the end of the eighteenth century, the French Revolution had begun in Europe the persecution of the Church and of her Religious Orders. This godless movement passed into Spain, and thence to her colonies, and the law of October, 1820, put into effect in Yucatán in 1821, suppressed the Franciscan Order. The *Convento Capitular* in Mérida was closed, and many of its possessions confiscated. It will be recalled that the convent in Mérida possessed an image of the Virgin identical to the one in the sanctuary at Izamal. So alike were these two images that they were often referred to as "the two sisters." Upon the suppression of the convent in Mérida in 1821, this image became the property of the Countess Doña Narcisa de la Cámara. When the Countess heard of the tragic event at Izamal, she offered her own statue to replace the one destroyed. The offer was accepted, and Our Lady of Izamal may be seen to this day in her shrine.

But there is one thing that the devout visitor to Our Lady of Izamal will not see. Deep within the breast of the venerable image, in the region where the heart would be, there is the figure of the Most Pure Heart of Mary, and set in it a tiny representation of her Crucified Son. And within the head, the organ of intelligence, are placed some texts from Sacred Scripture inscribed upon parchment. It is fitting that, from this centuries-old shrine and from this man-made image of Mary, token of the love of a people, there should ascend to the Eternal Throne, accompanying the prayers of Mary's children, the perpetual strains of the Magnificat.

XXIV

NUESTRA SANTISIMA MADRE DE LA LUZ

(OUR MOST HOLY MOTHER OF THE LIGHT)

León, Guanajuato

*T*HE town of León lies on the road between Mexico and El Paso, about two hundred and sixty miles from Mexico City. It is an old town, having been founded within years of the Conquest, and the Conquistador-founder named it after the province of León in his native Spain. It is a pretty town, on the old colonial model, with narrow streets and numerous tree-bowered plazas. And it is a religious town, with a number of fine churches, usually filled with reverent worshipers. The center of devotion in León is the fine cathedral, begun by the Jesuits in 1746 and partially completed before their expulsion from New Spain in 1767. The cathedral is also the sanctuary of a remarkable painting known as *Nuestra Santísima Madre de la Luz* ("Our Most Holy Mother of the Light"). It is the time-honored tradition of this greatly venerated image that we relate here.

Giovanni Antonio Genovesi was born in Palazzo Adriano in Sicily, the fourth of May, 1684, and became a novice in the Society of Jesus on the second of March, 1703. As a missionary for twenty years, he traversed in his apostolic labors the length and breadth of Sicily. During this period he gained countless souls for Christ through His Virgin Mother, under

La Madre SS. De La Luz

OUR MOST HOLY MOTHER OF THE LIGHT
León, Guanajuato

whose protection the missioner had placed his work. A man of heroic virtues and self-abnegation, he manifested in every breath he drew a great love for God. The conclusion of his life was a fitting climax to his work of apostolic charity. Appointed Master of Novices and Rector of the college at Messina, he was there when the great plague of 1743 struck. He turned the college into a hospital, and with exemplary Christian generosity the Jesuits selflessly and untiringly cared for the bodies and souls of the plague-smitten. One by one novices and their masters fell victims to the scourge, until finally only five remained; the others died in the arms of Father Genovesi. Himself ill, the Rector assumed the duty of cooking for all in the college. On the sixth of July, 1743, Father Genovesi too, as much a martyr to his burning love for souls as a victim of the plague, finally recommended his soul to God.

Such was the caliber of the man who introduced the devotion to Our Lady, Most Holy Mother of the Light. It is related that one day, in the course of his missionary travels, he arrived in Palermo. As was his wont, Father Genovesi placed the endeavor under the protection of the Blessed Virgin. In order that his preaching might bear more fruit, he decided to carry with him some image of her. But what image should it be; under what representation of her unparalleled virtues would Mary most deeply move the hearts and souls of his hearers?

At this time there was living in a convent of Palermo a very holy nun, whom the Blessed Virgin was accustomed to visit from time to time. Father Genovesi went to her and explained his problem. He wanted a painting of the Blessed Mother that would move the hearts of those who gazed upon it. And who would know better than Our Lady herself how the canvas should portray her? Therefore, besought Father

Genovesi, would the nun kindly ask the Blessed Mother to enlighten him on the matter?

The religious promised to ask the Most Holy Virgin for aid. One morning soon afterward, while the nun was absorbed in prayer, Our Lady appeared. She carried the Divine Infant, and was accompanied by a cortege of angels and a celestial retinue whose splendor was almost indescribable. "From the celestial presence there issued such a radiance of light," says an early writer, "that by comparison the sun appeared to be but a waxen taper." The astonished nun was almost overcome by this outstanding mark of Our Lady's predilection, and asked:

"Why, O Mother, do I see you today in such an extraordinary manner, surrounded by your heavenly court?"

"Have you forgotten," replied Mary, "the request you promised to make of me on behalf of one who earnestly appealed to you?"

And with that, Our Lady appeared in the act of snatching the soul of a sinner from the flaming jaws of hell, represented as a fearsome demon. The nun recalled that Father Genovesi had spoken of offering to Mary the hearts of sinners, to show that it was from her that their conversion must come. She related this to Our Lady, who nodded her assent. Then the apparition beckoned to one of the angels to kneel before her holding a basket of human hearts, and from it the Infant Jesus, on His Mother's arm, took the hearts one by one, sanctifying them by His touch.

"I wish the painting to be as you have seen me," said Our Lady, "and my invocation to be under the title, 'Most Holy Mother of the Light.'"

She repeated the command twice as if to emphasize it, and then vanished from sight.

The nun sent word to Father Genovesi, describing in detail how the painting was to be made, and he in turn commissioned an artist to execute it. But as neither nun nor missioner was able to be present during the actual painting, the work did not turn out satisfactorily. This is not to be wondered at, since the zealous missioner's verbal description of the holy nun's vision had to be translated to canvas by a third party. Consequently, the painting failed by far to measure up to the hopes of Father Genovesi. What was more important, it did not please the Blessed Virgin herself, as we shall now learn.

The pious nun of whom we have spoken lived at this period in a convent some distance from Palermo, where the artist had his studio. Given the times, and the nature of her vocation, we can see that under ordinary circumstances it would be well-nigh impossible for her to see the painting. But Our Blessed Mother did not view the case in this light. One day she appeared to the nun and gently chided her:

"What are you doing here, lazybones, at a time when I need you in Palermo for a matter which concerns my glory?"

"My Lady, such a useless servant as I could never be an instrument of your glory!" humbly answered the religious. "And who better than you knows the bonds which hold me chained here, so that I cannot take even one step toward any other place?"

"No matter," said the Blessed Virgin. "I wish to use you to bring this business of mine to a glorious conclusion. Go to Palermo, no matter how. Set out without delay. It will be the task of Divine Providence to resolve the difficulties or make them yield to a greater force."

Almost at once the nun was attacked by an asthmatic condition which scarcely permitted her to breathe, let alone speak. The physicians were unable to provide the slightest relief, and unanimously declared that she must be sent immediately to Palermo, where the milder, purer air would help her. Arrived in the city the nun experienced immediate relief, the mysterious attack ceasing as quickly as it had begun.

While still in Palermo, and desirous of seeing the painting of Our Most Holy Mother of the Light, she made arrangements with Father Genovesi to visit the artist's studio.

"Oh, no!" she exclaimed as soon as she glimpsed the picture. "That is not the form in which the Holy Virgin wants to be depicted. That isn't at all the way she let me see her!"

"So it seems to me, too," said Father Genovesi. "Will you, then, speak to the Virgin again, to find whether she wants a new painting, or whether this one may be retouched?"

The nun once more promised. A few days later, after Holy Communion, the Blessed Virgin appeared to her. Prostrate at Mary's feet, she poured out the story. "And so," she concluded, "we want to know whether you wish another picture to be painted."

The Virgin's response was made in a mild yet firm tone. She was not at all satisfied with the painting; the artist was to undertake another, to represent her exactly as she had previously appeared.

The religious lost no time in making this known to Father Genovesi. He for his part now petitioned her to beg Our Lady to appear in the artist's studio, so that the finished picture might carry out their intention. For many days the nun sent fervent prayers heavenward, and one morning, during her thanksgiving after Holy Communion, Our Lady reappeared. Once more she affirmed her desire to be painted according to the manner of that earlier appearance, and to be venerated with a special devotion under the title "Most Holy Mother of the Light."

"Now," she continued, "go to the painter, who is at this moment working in his studio. You will meet me there, and only you will see me. While you perceive me before you, make the necessary observations to the painter. I, though unseen, will guide the brush. When the work is completed, all shall know by its more than human beauty that a greater mind and a higher art have arranged the composition and laid the colors."

Full of joy, the nun betook herself to the artist's studio. He was already at work on the new canvas. Our Lady was there, too, visible to the religious in the same attitude in which she had ordered the painting to be done. With the celestial Lady invisibly guiding the brush strokes, and with the nun's directions giving exactness to the lineaments and fidelity to the colors, the image grew on the canvas as if by magic. So perfect and harmonious was the result that no copy, it is said, has ever been able to do justice to the original, though many eminent painters have essayed it. Even the original artist, tradition relates, many times in his later years tried in vain to recapture in colors that combination of majesty, devotion, and amiability which shows forth in his masterpiece.

The Queen of Heaven was well pleased with the finished picture. She examined it carefully, gracious and smiling the while. Then she raised her hand, and blessed the painting with the Sign of the Cross. According to Father Genovesi, it was through this blessing that Our Lady conferred upon her picture the virtue of "the continuing and stupendous miracles" thenceforward connected with devotion to Our Most Holy Mother of the Light.

For the remainder of his missionary life, Father Genovesi carried the painting on his journeys. Thanks to Our Mother of the Light, these missionary endeavors were rewarded by numerous conversions. Devotion to Our Lady under this spe-

cial title became intense throughout the length and breadth
of Sicily. When it was known that the zealous missioner and
his miraculous painting were to visit a particular town or village, the inhabitants outdid themselves in decorating their
churches and altars in Mary's honor. Deputations of clergy
and layfolk, with candles, flowers, and music, journeyed miles
along the road whence the missioner was expected, to welcome
our Most Holy Mother of the Light and her devoted legate.
According to tradition, so great was the love and devotion
which the image aroused that the faithful never willingly
parted with it. Thus arose the custom of leaving, at the end
of the mission, a faithful copy of the painting in the principal
church of the town, which was then placed under the protection of Our Lady, Mother of the Light.

How did the miraculous painting find its way from
Palermo in Sicily to León in far-off Mexico? This latter part of
the story is connected with another Jesuit of almost the same
family name: José María Genovese.

Father Genovese, also a native of Sicily, reached the shores
of Mexico in 1707. Some time after the painting of the sacred
picture in 1722, having learned of the devotion, he erected
many altars dedicated to Our Lady under the title "Mother
of the Light." By 1732, according to the most popular tradition,
the original painting found its way into his hands. This faithful servant of God became renowned for the devotion to Our
Lady. By the time of his death in 1757, he had labored fifty-
eight years as a member of the Society of Jesus. During his
later life he had many copies of the painting made and dis-
tributed throughout Mexico, to foster devotion to the Virgin
under the advocation "Mother of the Light."

José María Genovese wished that the devotion to Our
Most Holy Mother of the Light should be as fervent and

widespread in Mexico as it was in Sicily. To this end he decided in 1732 to place the painting in one of the many churches which the Jesuits had at that time in New Spain. But which one? It might have seemed that some of the more ancient of the Jesuit foundations, notably the famous *Iglesia de la Profesa* in Mexico City, had a claim to special consideration. But Father Genovese was not to be influenced by purely historical facts. He decided to choose the new sanctuary of Our Lady in Biblical fashion, by drawing lots. All the churches which the Society had in its Province of Mexico were included in the drawing, and the choice fell upon the newest foundation, the hospice of León, scarcely a year old. Could it be possible that Our Lady wanted her image to remain there? But a second drawing, and then a third, confirmed the will of God in the matter.

On the second of July, 1732, the venerable image arrived at León in triumph. At first it reposed in the Jesuit church later known as *La Santa Escuela*. In 1767, when the Jesuits were expelled from New Spain, they left behind a magnificent church, well on the way to completion, which today is the cathedral church of León. It is here that the painting is venerated today, having been transferred from its earlier sanctuary in 1864.

In 1849, the civil and religious authorities took solemn oath to hold Our Most Holy Mother of the Light as chief Patroness of the city, and when León became a diocese in 1872, Our Lady was chosen diocesan Patroness under this same title. Each year on the second of July, the anniversary of the painting's arrival is celebrated in León, as the city comes alive with *fiesta*. Pope Leo XIII, on the twenty-second of March, 1891, signed a Brief approving the Pontifical Coronation of the image by the Diocese of León. The crowning took place on the eighth of October, 1902.

Through the years, one writer after another has recorded
the signal favors granted to León by Our Most Holy Mother
of the Light. To her intercession has been attributed protection from storms, lightning, and plagues. In thanksgiving
for having been saved from the cholera epidemic of 1850,
the people of León promised a solemn triduum of prayer annually on the three days preceding the Feast of the Assumption, the fifteenth of August. Our Lady is also credited with
protecting León from invasion during the various wars and
revolutions which have beset Mexico. During the War of
Independence of 1810, Our Lady was proclaimed official De-
fender of León, and invested with the *bastón* of gold and the
red sash of a commanding general. In fact, León has enjoyed
such outstanding peace during the various revolutions that it
is also known as "The City of Refuge," a name conferred
upon it by grateful Mexicans who found sanctuary within its
walls.

A favorite story of Our Lady's predilection for the city is
told by the people of León. At eleven forty-five on the morning of the eighteenth of June, 1876, the cathedral was filled
with worshipers at Sunday Mass. Suddenly the keystone of
the main arch, a tremendous block of masonry, fell into the
aisle. Not a person was injured! A panic of major proportions might have ensued if the accident had occurred elsewhere. With great presence of mind and sublime faith, Bishop Diez de Sollano walked down and stood under the arch,
and before his flock, prayed to Our Most Holy Mother of the
Light to hold up the arch and save her sanctuary. The prayer
was heard, and in gratitude the saintly bishop built and dedicated to Our Lady the jewel-like little chapel known as the
Holy House of Loreto, next door to the cathedral.

Not only in León, however, but throughout the Republic
of Mexico, Our Most Holy Mother of the Light has her faith-

ful devotees. Her image may be met with in the the most modern city and in the humblest pueblo, in hacienda chapel and on *jacal* wall. Taxis and buses in León are commonly fitted up with little shrines to *Nuestra Santísima Madre de la Luz* surrounded by colored lights, and burly, hard-bitten truck drivers carry her picture affixed to the cab dashboard. Furthermore, this title of Mary is one of the two most popular names given to girls in baptism: one is "Lupe," for *Santa María de Guadalupe;* the other, "Luz," for *Nuestra Santísima Madre de la Luz.*

XXV

NUESTRA SEÑORA DEL CARMEN

(OUR LADY OF MOUNT CARMEL)

Tlalpujahuac, Mexico

*I*T IS a dusty train ride or a rugged auto trip by an indifferent road to Tlalpujahuac, in the northwestern corner of the State of Mexico. In years gone by it was the center of the richest gold mining district of New Spain. Long before the Spanish Conquistadors set foot in the New World, the Mazahua Indians had worked the area for its glittering treasure. But when the Spaniards and other Europeans arrived, they exploited the mines to a fantastic degree. The fabulous José de la Borda, that almost legendary Frenchman who came to Mexico in 1716, is said to have taken over ten million dollars in gold out of his mines in Tlalpujahuac alone.

There was a parish in Tlalpujahuac as early as 1567, but the church was poorly constructed and soon fell into ruins. A later church, however, built in the era of José de la Borda, was a masterpiece of sumptuosity, and has a rather curious history. According to tradition, the fabulous Frenchman told the townsfolk of Tlalpujahuac that he would build them a new parish church at his own expense. The authorities regarded the gesture of this foreigner with a certain degree of distrust, and asked him to give a bond which would guarantee fulfillment of the undertaking. Don José considered the

OUR LADY OF MOUNT CARMEL
Tlalpujahuac, Mexico

suggestion a reflection on his honor, and refused the request, so the townsfolk undertook to finance the project without the French capitalist's help. Now Borda had other mines of silver, notably in Taxco and Zacatecas, which had brought him another twenty-five million dollars. To show that he was able to carry out his promise, he proceeded to construct at his own expense the almost unbelievably magnificent church of Santa Prisca in Taxco, today one of the wonders of Mexico. Alongside it, the church in Tlalpujahuac, though richly ornamented and appointed, looks rather modest.

In the 1890's and the first years of the twentieth century, Tlalpujahuac was a hustling, prosperous mining camp town, sharing in the wealth of its neighbor El Oro, crowded with American engineers and mine bosses and their families. Today the gold of Tlalpujahuac is exhausted, and the town is a lethargic, down-at-heel old place, well on the way to becoming a ghost town.

Nevertheless, to the comparative handful of souls that remain, Tlalpujahuac is filled with memories of former days. Legends of the Conquistadors are still told around the plaza in the soft spring evenings, and the all-too-occasional visitor has pointed out to him the famous bonanzas of olden times. And there is one never-failing source of interest to the student of religious traditions, the collector of Mariana, and the devout client of Mary. That is the legendary shrine erected in honor of Our Lady of Carmel just outside the city walls at the beginning of the sixteenth century. In former times it was the repository of an image of *Nuestra Señora del Carmel* ("Our Lady of Mount Carmel"), painted upon the adobe wall.

No one is quite certain of the origin of this image. We do know, though, that the Catholic Otomí and Mazahua Indians had the pious custom of constructing little shrines or oratories in honor of their *santos,* or favorite patrons. There was a flourishing trade in the making of religious sculpture and paintings; scarcely a *pueblito* or *rancho* in the region that did not have its quota of such sanctuaries.

The construction of such an oratory was an event of paramount importance in the life of a family. When the head of a family decided to build an oratory, he invited some important figure in the region, often a Spanish Crown official or a *hacendado,* to become his *compadre,* that is, patron, in the enterprise. When this occurred, a religious and economic relationship was formed between the two similar to that assumed between subject and godfather in baptism, and this regardless of differences in social status. It constituted a solemn and lasting union. From the first ground-breaking for the new construction, through the laying of the cornerstone, to the final blessing by the local pastor or missionary *padre,* each phase of the work was marked by the observance of definite religious ceremonies. When the oratory was completed, the care of it was solemnly bequeathed from father to son, and likewise the patronal obligation might be handed down through the family of the *compadre.*

In the eighteenth century a certain Don Felipe Neri Valleza had an official inquiry made among the natives in the region of Tlalpujahuac, to ascertain what they knew of the earlier history of this image of Our Lady of Carmel. The inquiry uncovered some interesting local traditions. It seems that a chapel for the celebration of Mass was constructed upon the hacienda of the proprietor of a local silver mine. On the walls were painted representations of various saints, following the practice of the Carmelites in their convents and churches. One of these paintings was the image of Our Lady of Mount Carmel.

Generations passed by; the hacienda was abandoned and at length fell into ruins. The roof of the chapel caved in, and the images on the walls were exposed to the dust storms and the summer rains. Finally only the image of Our Lady remained to recall the devotion of former times.

One evening, a group of the local residents were amusing themselves at cards in the house of a certain José de Mendieta. One of his neighbors came running in with an exciting tale. He had stopped at the ruined chapel nearby, to pray to Our Lady of Carmel, but the image had disappeared from the wall! José de Mendieta and his friends went immediately by torchlight to examine the phenomenon, but when they arrived at the chapel, they found the painting where it had always been. Since their informant was a reliable man, they concluded that there was some mystery connected with the happening. Perhaps Our Lady was sending them a special message. At all events, as devout men, they decided to build a new chapel to house the painting of Our Lady.

When the chapel was completed, they contracted with several artists to brighten the colors of the image. To the surprise of the artists, whereas the paint of the clothing was badly damaged, the features were so fresh and brilliant that no retouching of them was necessary. This fact was certified later by the pastor and by many people from the mining camp. A deposition made at the same time mentions numerous favors obtained through the sacred image.

In later years a new chapel of solid masonry was built, and the adobe wall containing Our Lady's image was placed in the sanctuary above the main altar.

When, in 1903, a raging fire destroyed the sanctuary, the image was preserved from the flames in an extraordinary fashion. However, funds were not available for rebuilding, and it was feared that the temple would have to remain in ruins. Suddenly, a new and rich vein was discovered in the

Dos Estrellas mine at El Oro, and with the revival of prosperity the sanctuary was restored.

On the sixteenth of May, 1930, the solemn coronation of Our Lady of Tlalpujahuac took place. The gold crown which today rests upon the head of the statue is a duplicate of the original, stolen some time ago by sacrilegious hands.

On the twenty-seventh of May, 1937, a catastrophe occurred in Tlalpujahuac, in which the image of Our Lady was marvelously preserved. At twenty minutes past five in the morning, a large dam gave way, pouring the cyanide-filled tailings of mining operations down upon the sanctuary. In the space of about ten minutes some hundreds of thousands of tons of tailings had poured into the district, filling the church to a height of twenty-seven feet, and in other places rising to one hundred and ten feet. After taking care of the victims of the catastrophe, the pastor devoted himself to directing rescue operations for Our Lady's image. The difficult task involved cutting through the walls, removing the three-hundred-year-old adobe, and carrying it over a rocky ledge more than half a mile in a pounding rainstorm. In spite of all, the image was finally brought unharmed to the parish church. There it reposes today, over the principal altar, a reminder of the faith and devotion of the pueblo, and a witness to the love of Our Lady of Mount Carmel for her people of Tlalpujahuac.

OUR LADY OF THE ROUND CHURCH
Mexico, D. F.

SANTA MARIA LA REDONDA

(OUR LADY OF THE ROUND CHURCH)

Mexico, D. F.

cA SHORT time before the founding of Tenochtitlán by the Aztecs, the city later to be known as Mexico was divided into four main sections, or barrios — according to tradition, by Huitzilopochtli. These four sections were based upon their relationship to the Great Temple, on whose site, now the politico-geographical center of Mexico, stands the metropolitan cathedral. These four sections were: the northern, *Cuepopan,* or "Place Where the Flowers Bloom"; the eastern, *Teopan,* or "Place of the God" (that is, place where the sun rises); the southern, *Moyotlan,* "Place of Mosquitos" (because of the canals and marshes); and the western, *Axtacalco,* "Place of the Herons." The Spaniards, throughout the entire colonial period, maintained this same division of the city into four great districts or barrios. They did, however, change their names to others with a Christian significance. *Teopan* became San Pablo; *Moyotlan* was christened San Juan; *Axtacalco* became San Sebastián; *Cuepopan* was changed to Santa María la Redonda.

Each of these four main districts was in turn subdivided into calpullis, or lesser barrios. The individual barrios were

devoted, at least in a number of cases, to special trades or in-
dustries. The barrio of Amantlán, for example, was occupied
by artisans who specialized in the fabrication of feather
mosaics, now virtually a lost art.

The sixteenth-century Church of Santa María la Redonda
stands in the center of the district which, even today, bears
its name. The main avenue through the district is called likewise Santa María la Redonda; at the south end it becomes San
Juan Letrán, once the principal thoroughfare of the southern
barrio of San Juan, and today the center of the middle-class
shopping district of Mexico.

In early Spanish times the calpulli in which the church
stands was known as Tlaquechchiuhcan, from the Nahuatl
word *tlaquechtli* ("matting"), and signified "the place where
they make mattresses." The Church of Santa María la Redonda was founded there by Fray Pedro de Gante in 1524,
and dedicated to the Assumption of the Blessed Virgin Mary.
It was one of those in charge of the Franciscan Order, and
on Sundays and holydays of obligation a Franciscan would
come from the chapel of San José to offer Mass. On the
patronal Feast of the Assumption a procession went through
the streets of the barrio, and all the confraternities, carrying
their banners, took part.

It is related that one year, while the Indians were going
in procession, some students from the nearby seminary, with
the thoughtlessness of youth, began to make fun of them. The
good natives, who took their religion very seriously, became in-
censed. They broke the line of march and charged their
tormentors. Soon a full-fledged riot was in progress. There
was a curious sequel to the fracas. The Archbishop issued an
edict forbidding both students and members of the secular
clergy to be spectators of the procession, and this under penalty
of excommunication!

A *Real Cédula* dated the fifteenth of November, 1598, gave to the Franciscans His Majesty's permission for a house of studies and a novitiate there, and three thousand pesos from the royal treasury were earmarked for the necessary construction, and for assisting in the care of the required Indian workers. The Franciscans put the convent under the direction of their Commissary General, who then had the right to name its Guardian. Also, and importantly, the religious were granted the right to choose their own civil patron.

A certain Diego Juarez de Peredo offered to accept the patronage, with its accompanying financial responsibilities, under certain conditions. He wished to dedicate an altar to his patron saint in the Convent of San Francisco in Mexico, and one in the chapel in Tulancingo, with the privilege of having Mass offered annually for his intention at each one. These conditions were accepted, and Don Diego then built the staircase and a dormitory, after which a Franciscan went into residence. But at this point, apparently, either Don Diego's money, or his interest, or his piety gave out. At any rate, the construction came to a halt and was never resumed, so the house of studies never became an actuality. The next patron was the Conde del Valle, but he likewise gave up the honor after a while. Consequently his coat of arms, which had been displayed prominently above the doorkeeper's lodge in stone, was chiseled off. From then on the Franciscans assumed the responsibility themselves. There were then five religious, including the Minister of the convent, who also acted as pastor of the church. Around the turn of the eighteenth century the census numbered about eight hundred souls. It seems to have been an active little community, as the parish had five lay confraternities. The two principal ones, of the Blessed Sacrament and of Our Lady of the Assumption, each had a High Mass once a month. The Confraternities of the

Holy Sepulcher, the Dormition, and the Souls in Purgatory each had a High Mass every other week.

The building has undergone several periods of reconstruction during the seventeenth and eighteenth centuries. The church has a curiously circular appearance, caused by the form of the apse and the *camarín*. It was this which gave the church, and consequently the barrio, its name: *Santa María la Redonda* ("Saint Mary the Round"). Another distinctive feature is a "leaning tower," an intriguing octagonal structure built into one of the side walls, and matched by a counterfort of the same form on the other side. There is an attached cloister, ancient and interesting, where today the *notario* (parish secretary) transacts the parish business. The church building was declared a national monument in 1932, and so is actually the property of the Mexican government. This makes for a curious dichotomy of functions, since the custodian is a government official who opens and locks the church at stated hours, and not even the pastor may enter without his permission.

An ancient image, called *Nuestra Señora de la Redonda,* has been venerated there since the early seventeenth century. Fray Rodrigo de Zequera, Commissary General of the Franciscans, sent from Spain to the Convent of La Redonda the face and hands for a statue of Our Lady. This was quite a common practice, especially after the custom of vesting images had become widespread in New Spain. The Guardian of the convent showed the treasure to his people, and one of them, an old Indian woman, offered to have an image of the Virgin made. According to a legend, when she took the pieces home, she found three men awaiting her. They introduced themselves as officials who also were expert craftsmen, and offered to make the statue for her. The good woman gratefully accepted the offer, and assigned them quarters in her house where they might carry out their task. They worked for three days. On the fourth morning, when the matron went to their apartment to see how the labor was faring, she found to her surprise that the artisans had gone, leaving the image completed. And such an image! Instead of the crude and unfinished outlines usually to be found in the torso and limbs of statues designed, as this one presumably was to have been, to be vested in fabric, the image was beautifully sculptured its entire length. Even the features, which had originally been in frontal perspective, had been foreshortened with consummate artistry to blend with the general outlines of the image, and the eyes were now turned heavenward, as if to signify that the image had come from above. Overcome with admiration, the pious woman had the statue carried to La Redonda. The early chronicler of the legend relates that the image was venerated for its beauty as a miracle of art, or as a work of art wrought by a miracle.

On Monday evening in Holy Week the image was carried in procession through the city by torchlight, accompanied by the religious of the Franciscan community, members of the Third Order in their habits, and many of the diocesan clergy. As the procession threaded its way through the streets, flowers would be showered down from the balconies and windows upon the image, and bands of musicians would serenade the Virgin and then join the ever-growing train of devotees.

Numerous miracles are attributed by the faithful to the intercession of *Nuestra Señora de la Redonda*. Mexico at the time of the Conquest was at the mercy of those dread scourges of urban life, disease, fire, and lack of water. Often the three went hand in hand. In the native barrios, the flimsy construction of the dwellings could turn any small blaze into a major conflagration which, during the dry season, would

burn unchecked. The shortage of water and the faulty drain-
age often led to deadly epidemics.

In the year 1670 there was an extreme scarcity of rain, even
for a climate where there is virtually no rain for six months
out of the year. The parishioners of La Redonda requested a
license to hold a procession with the image for the purpose of
praying for rain. The Dean of the cathedral, Don Juan de
Poblete, who was Archbishop-elect of Manila, approved the
petition, and the necessary license was then granted by the
civil authorities. The *Real Provisor* who issued the license,
however, laid down a restriction: the procession might go
only as far as the neighboring parish of Santa Catalina, turning down the Calle San Lorenzo. On the ninth of July, while
the procession was in progress, a heavy shower occurred — so
heavy that the bearers were forced to take the image into the
Convent of San Lorenzo for protection. Now here is the
strange part of the story: the rain confined itself to that part
of the Calle San Lorenzo through which the procession had
passed! The rest of the city remained without a drop of rain,
as if to show that the Virgin was displeased by the edict.

Another very colorful legend among the many associated
with *Nuestra Señora de la Redonda* concerns the old church
of San Augustín. On the eleventh of December, 1676, a fire
broke out there, of such intensity that the lead used in the
roofing came pouring through the rain gutters in molten
streams, and cooling at the base, stoppered the drainpipes.
The image of the Virgin was hurriedly brought from the
church of La Redonda. When the statue neared the blazing
building, it is related, the flames ceased at once, as though at
a command. On this occasion an impromptu procession of
thanksgiving was formed, and over three thousand persons
carrying candles and torches lighted the Virgin back to her
shrine.

In the year 1696 another striking instance of the Virgin's power over the elements was manifested. During the first fourteen days of June, not a drop of rain had fallen in the city. On the fifteenth, the wonder-working image was carried in procession from the Convent of Santa Isabel to the cathedral, with the Viceroy and the Canons of the cathedral chapter taking part, together with members of all the religious orders. At the cathedral a solemn novena of prayer was instituted. When the novena was concluded, the image was taken in procession to the Convent of Santa Clara, and thereupon rain fell in such abundance that the cisterns and reservoirs were overflowing.

Today the district of Santa María la Redonda is pretty much of a slum area: old and run-down dwellings with a fringe of untidy shops. The main thoroughfare, with the gracious name of the district's Patroness, is a roaring, noisy, crowded highway, filled with industrial and business traffic, lumbering trucks and darting taxis, shabby *bodegas* and cafés, and tawdry places of amusement. Yet barely two minutes away, in a quiet little street, is the spiritual heart of this teeming district, and here one can turn back the clock three hundred years. Here the noises of the twentieth century reach one strangely muted, and within an ironwork gate a grass-lined walk leads to the church's door. At its left, a weatherworn inscription commemorating the foundation is no longer decipherable. But somehow that does not seem important now. What matters is the Truth within those doors: the Presence signaled by the glow of a sanctuary lamp, and she whose loving care for the little folk of Santa María is figured by a magnificently sculptured image of the Assumption.

THE TEMPLE OF SANTO DOMINGO

Mexico, D. F.

*W*HEN the first Dominicans arrived in Mexico on the twenty-fourth of July, 1526, the Franciscans offered them the fraternal hospitality of their own Convent of San Francisco. By October of the same year the Dominican *frailes* had acquired a small residence at the northeast corner of today's Plazuela de Santo Domingo. Around this plaza, for more than four hundred years now, much of the civil and religious life of Mexico has flowed. For one thing, the site of their first residence is now occupied by the imposing building that housed the Tribunal of the Holy Office (also known as the Inquisition), which we might call a kind of religious watchdog in matters of faith and morals. The building used by the Holy Office is today the National School of Medicine. Across the street from it, and facing down along the plaza toward the cathedral, is the mother church of the Dominican Order in Mexico: Santo Domingo. This church is doubtless one of the finest in the capital, as well as one of the oldest in point of foundation. The original church was built in 1571, but, because of the sinking of the city — still a very serious problem — it was, by 1607, almost nine feet out of the perpendicular. Philip II ordered it restored, but by 1716 it had

182

OUR LADY OF THE ROSARY

sunk again and the lower part had filled with water; consequently it had to be rebuilt from the foundations. The new structure, the present-day church, was completed in 1736, and consecrated in 1754 by a Dominican bishop, Fray Francisco Pallas, the Vicar-Apostolic of Fokien. This church is considered one of the finest examples of Baroque architecture in Mexico, and, with its stately façade, finely proportioned dome, and spacious Roman vault soaring from its single nave, merits more than a brief description or a casual visit. But our concern here is primarily with the shrines of Our Lady which the temple contains, and it is to a consideration of them that we now turn.

Fortunate is the church which possesses an image of Our Lady; more fortunate still the church which holds one of Mary's images renowned for its antiquity, the devotion which it inspires, and a well-authenticated tradition of remarkable favors granted there. What, then, are we to say of the temple of Santo Domingo, which possesses not one but two of these renowned shrines of Our Lady? One is the shrine to Our Lady of the Rosary; the other, to Our Lady of Covadonga.

NUESTRA SEÑORA DEL ROSARIO

The Dominican Order is, by tradition, the first recipient of the Rosary, through its saintly founder, from the hands of Our Blessed Lady; the temple of Santo Domingo is the mother church of the Order in Mexico. The shrine of Our Lady of the Rosary in Santo Domingo must therefore be numbered first among the Rosary shrines in the Republic; it is fitting that it should be among the most beautiful and most magnificently adorned of the shrines in the New World. A shrine where everything is of gold except the silver globe upon which Mary stands, it yet serves merely as a setting for its

principal treasure, a jewel-like figure of Our Lady of the
Rosary. Life-size, and fashioned with exquisite artistry, Our
Lady of the Rosary seems to be a living person. The eyes
appear to move, the figure to respire, and the face to be alight
with a thousand changes of expression. Even the Infant on
His Mother's arm looks down as though He were about to
speak.

La Capilla del Rosario — the Rosary Chapel — was built
to replace an earlier one that stood outside the church, within
the old cloister, now gone. The high wall of the *claustro* was
demolished and the old chapel severed from the church when
a street was cut through the monastery grounds.

La Capilla del Rosario is the shrine and spiritual headquarters for the Confraternity of the Most Holy Rosary. It
was founded the sixteenth of March, 1538, only a few years
after Cortés conquered the armies of Mocteczuma; few
associations can boast such celebrated membership or such
a glorious history. The Dominican chronicler, Fray Juan José
Moya, writing in 1757, affirms that already at that time the
work of the Confraternity of the Rosary was remarkable.
Let us consider several of their charitable enterprises. One of
these dealt with a dowry for orphaned girls of Spanish families. Because of reverses of fortune, many a young woman
of good family would be left penniless upon the death of her
parent or guardian, and, dowerless, be unable to find a husband of her own class. *La Cofradía del Santísimo Rosario*
undertook to provide every year a dowry of three hundred
pesos to each of twenty orphaned girls of marriageable age.
In addition, Padre Moya noted, the Confraternity had in-
vestments of over two million pesos, the income from which
was devoted to works of charity.

OUR LADY OF COVADONGA

Members of the Confraternity of the Rosary bind themselves to recite the fifteen Mysteries of the Rosary every week. In return they gain innumerable Indulgences.

The devotion of the "Perpetual Rosary" also has its headquarters at the shrine, and at any hour that the temple is open, one may see several people at the priedieux before the altar, rosary in hand. In its primitive form, the devotion of the Perpetual Rosary consisted in each member's giving one hour a year, at a definite time, to this prayer. In 1896 the Perpetual Rosary was re-established according to a revised system, so that now there are a number of "divisions" within Mexico City, and others in the great cities throughout the Republic. The Guards of Honor of the Perpetual Rosary are all members of the Confraternity. In addition to their regular Confraternity obligation, each is assigned a specific hour and day every month to recite the entire fifteen mysteries of the Rosary.

On the fourteenth of October, 1945, by authority of His Holiness Pius XII and in his name, the coronation of Our Lady of the Rosary with the pontifical crown took place in the temple of Santo Domingo. There she reigns today, in a golden chapel, the crown gracing her brow, and a little silver world beneath her feet, to receive the homage of her subjects. *Salve Regina!*

NUESTRA SEÑORA DE COVADONGA

Nuestra Señora de Covadonga — "OUR LADY OF COVADONGA" — is an image of remarkable beauty representing Our Blessed Mother holding her Divine Son. Devotion to Our Lady of Covadonga is of considerable antiquity, Spanish in origin, and dating back to the time of the Crusades. Our Lady of Covadonga is the patroness of the Spaniards

in the Province of the Asturias, from whence the devotion
subsequently spread throughout Spain. A number of Asturians
were counted among the Conquistadors, and to them we owe
the translation of Our Lady of Covadonga to New Spain.
As the work of colonization flourished, more and more Spaniards came to Mexico, among them many of the devout and
aristocratic Asturians. By the middle of the eighteenth century, these devotees of Our Lady of Covadonga were substantial in both numbers and influence in the capital. At first
the image was venerated in the sixteenth-century church of
Valvanera in Mexico City, frequented by the Asturians. From
that church, with its *mudéjar* tower, so reminiscent of their
homeland, the image of Our Lady of Covadonga was transferred to the temple of Santo Domingo.

At the request of the Asturian population, *La Congregación de Nuestra Señora de Covadonga* was erected in Santo
Domingo on the twenty-ninth of January, 1785. At first membership in this Congregation was limited to Asturians resident
in Mexico. Later, as devotion to this advocation of Our Lady
became even more widespread, membership requirements were
broadened to admit all Spaniards and members of their families. On the thirteenth of September, 1896, the *Asociación
de Covadonga,* as it was henceforth to be known, was restored.
It continues to this day. Its object is to render homage to the
Virgin in gratitude for the benefits which she has bestowed
on Spain and its colonies, past and present. The members
are pledged to pray daily ten *Ave Marias,* and the fourth
Sunday of each month is set aside for special devotions in
Our Lady's honor. At one time this Association was one of
the wealthiest among the religious organizations of the laity
in Mexico. Fray Juan de la Cruz y Moya, speaking of the
altar of Our Lady of Covadonga, called it "the most perfect,

the finest, work in this Republic because of the devotion of the noble Asturian people, who endowed it with largesse."

The altar of Our Lady of Covadonga is an inspired mass of richly carved wood, of such size that it completely fills the chancel on the Gospel side of the church. This altar, in the Churrigueresque style, has a wealth of paintings and figurines, as well as a number of pieces of sculpture in highly ornamented niches. The gold with which all is covered gleams dully now beneath the patina of time, in the faint light that filters through the high stained-glass windows of the nave.

The image of Our Lady of Covadonga reposes in the central niche high above her altar. Sculptured in Spain in the late sixteenth or early seventeenth century, it is of wood, with the *peana,* or base *estofada,* polychromed and gilt. The Virgin is represented in her Divine Maternity; the Infant Christ is held on the left arm, and in the right hand are a rose and royal scepter. Robes of silk on both Mother and Child are richly worked in pearls and thread of pure gold, and bordered with gold lace. Both figures wear crowns of gold, and the Infant holds in His left hand the golden globe of empire. Slightly smaller than life size, the figures are masterpieces of beauty, especially that of the Virgin, on whose face is an expression of sublimity, timelessness, majesty. *Tota pulchra es, Maria!*

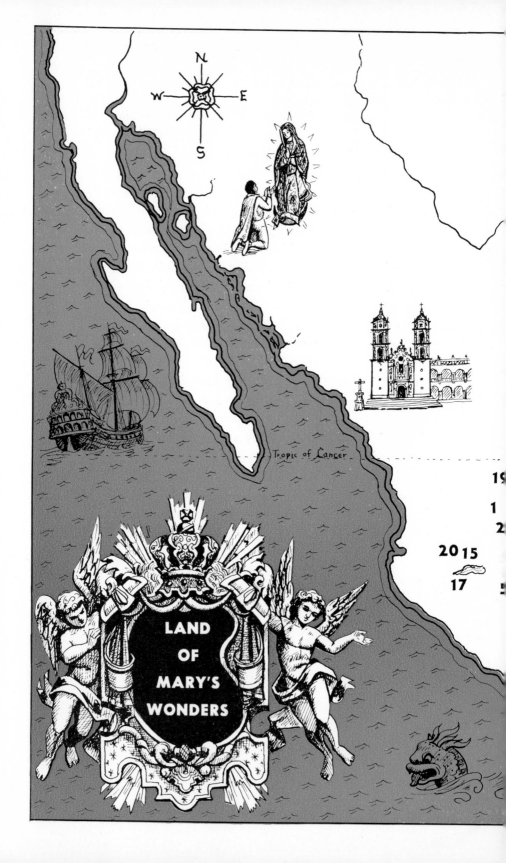

Tropic of Cancer

LAND
OF
MARY'S
WONDERS

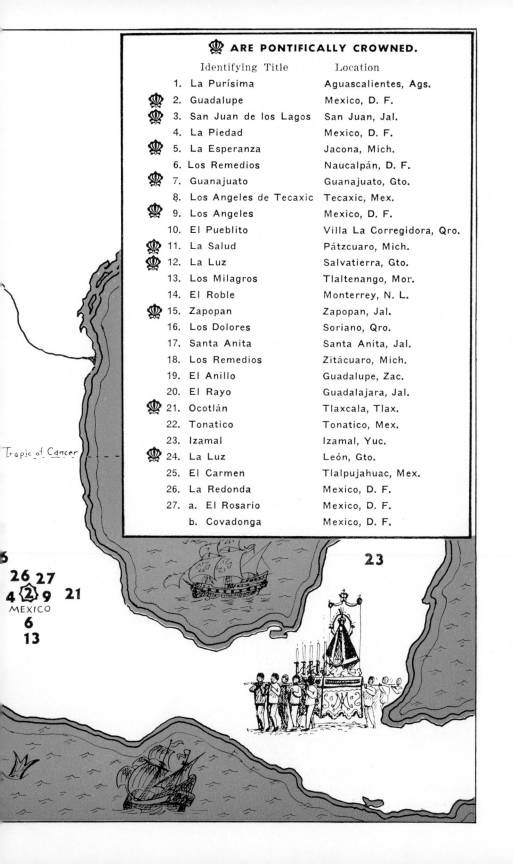

🌸 ARE PONTIFICALLY CROWNED.

	Identifying Title	Location
	1. La Purísima	Aguascalientes, Ags.
🌸	2. Guadalupe	Mexico, D. F.
🌸	3. San Juan de los Lagos	San Juan, Jal.
	4. La Piedad	Mexico, D. F.
🌸	5. La Esperanza	Jacona, Mich.
	6. Los Remedios	Naucalpán, D. F.
🌸	7. Guanajuato	Guanajuato, Gto.
	8. Los Angeles de Tecaxic	Tecaxic, Mex.
🌸	9. Los Angeles	Mexico, D. F.
	10. El Pueblito	Villa La Corregidora, Qro.
🌸	11. La Salud	Pátzcuaro, Mich.
🌸	12. La Luz	Salvatierra, Gto.
	13. Los Milagros	Tlaltenango, Mor.
	14. El Roble	Monterrey, N. L.
🌸	15. Zapopan	Zapopan, Jal.
	16. Los Dolores	Soriano, Qro.
	17. Santa Anita	Santa Anita, Jal.
	18. Los Remedios	Zitácuaro, Mich.
	19. El Anillo	Guadalupe, Zac.
	20. El Rayo	Guadalajara, Jal.
🌸	21. Ocotlán	Tlaxcala, Tlax.
	22. Tonatico	Tonatico, Mex.
	23. Izamal	Izamal, Yuc.
🌸	24. La Luz	León, Gto.
	25. El Carmen	Tlalpujahuac, Mex.
	26. La Redonda	Mexico, D. F.
	27. a. El Rosario	Mexico, D. F.
	b. Covadonga	Mexico, D. F.

Tropic of Cancer

23

6

26 27
4 (2) 9   21
MEXICO
6
13

ANONYMOUS, *Novena en Honor de la Santísima Virgen del Santuario de Tonatico, Edo. de Mexico.* Toluca, Mex., 1954.

BECERRA TANCO, Pbro. Luis, *Nuestra Señora de Guadalupe y Origen de su milagrosa Imagen.* Reimp. de la 1a. ed. de 1666, Mexico City, 1883.

BERRUECOS, José C., S. J., *Apuntes Historicos sobre la Imagen de Nuestra Señora de los Angeles y su Santuario.* 2a. Ed., Mexico, D. F., 1923.

CARRILLO y ANCONA, Dn. Crescencio, *La Civilización Yucateca.* Merida, Yucatán, 1949.

FLORENCIA, R. P. Francisco de, S. J., *Zodiaco Mariano.* Mexico City, 1755.

GARCIA GUTIERREZ, Dn. Jesús, *Datos Historicos sobre la Venerable Imagen de Nuestra Señora de los Remedios de Mexico.* 2a. Ed., Mexico, D. F., 1940.

GARCIA ICAZBALCETA, Dn. Joaquín, *Carta acerca del origen de la Imagen de Nuestra Señora de Guadalupe de Mexico.* Mexico City, 1896.

ISLA, Ezequiel de la, *Breves Apuntes Historicos acerca de la milagrosa Imagen de Nuestra Señora de los Dolores de Soriano.* Querétaro, Qro., 1947.

LIZANA, Fray Bernardo de, *Historia de Yucatán y Devocionario de Nuestra Señora de Izamal.* Impr. 1633. 2a Ed., Museo Nacional de Mexico.

LOPEZ BELTRÁN, Pbro. Lauro, *La Virgen de Tlaltenango.* Cuernavaca, Mor., 1950.

MARQUEZ, Dn. Pedro María, *Historia de Nuestra Señora de San Juan de los Lagos.* Mexico, D. F., 1939.

MENDIETA, FRAY JERÓNIMO DE, O. F. M., *Historia Eclesiástica Indiana.* Ed. J. G. Icazbalceta, Mexico, 1870.

MENDOZA, R. P. Fray Juan de, O. F. M., *Relación de la milagrosa Imagen de Nuestra Señora de los Angeles de Tecaxic.* Mexico City, 1684.

MIRELES, Pbro. Olegario, *Florilegio Mariano en honor de Nuestra Madre Santísima de la Luz.* Part III, León, Guanajuato, 1952.

MOJICA, Fray José Francisco de Guadalupe, O. F. M., *Documentos Historicos sobre la Sagrada Imagen de Nuestra Señora de la Luz.* Salvatierra, Guanajuato, 1939.

———, *El Indio y María Inmaculada.* Mexico, D. F., 1946.

191

OCHOA, Fray Angel S., O. F. M., *Breve Historia de Nuestra Señora ·Refugio de Pecadores.* San Luis Potosí, 1939.

——, *Breve Historia de la Purisima de San Diego de Aguascalientes.* Zapopan, Jal., 1953.

OROZCO, Pbro. Luis Enrique, *Iconografía Mariana de la Arquidoócesis de Guadalajara.* Tom. I, Guadalajara, Jalisco, 1954.

de PADUA, Antonio María, *La Madre de Dios en Mexico.* 2 Vols., Mexico City, 1888.

de PALACIO BASAVE, Fray Luis del Refugio, O. F. M., *Breve Historia de Nuestra Señora de Zapopan.* 2a. Ed., Guadalajara, Jal., 1950.

PALACIOS, R. P. Restituto A., C. SS. R., *Nuestra Señora del Perpetuo Socorro.* Mexico, D. F., 1949.

PUENTE CAMACHO, Esteban, *La Estrella del Sur: Historia de la Santísima Virgen de la Piedad.* Mexico, D. F., 1946.

QUIROZ y GUTIERREZ, Nicanor, *Historia de la Aparición de Nuestra Señora de Ocotlán.* Puebla, Pue., 1940.

RAMIREZ, Pbro. José Ysaac, *Manual de las Bases de la Congregación de Nuestra Señora de Guanajuato.* Guanajuato, Gto., 1900.

RICARD, ROBERT, *La Conquête Spirituelle du Mexique.* Paris, 1933.

ROBLES MARTÍNEZ, Luis, *Historia de la Imagen de Nuestra Señora del Rayo.* 3a. Ed. (rev.), Guadalajara, Jal., 1948.

RUIZ, R. P. Fray Pascual, O. F. M., *El Anillo de la Virgen de Guadalupe de Zacatecas.* Guadalajara, Jal., 1944.

RUIZ de ALARCON, Can. Dn. José Mariano, *Sermón de Nuestra Señora de Guadalupe.* Mexico, 1819.

SAHAGÚN, FRAY BERNARDINO DE, O. F. M., *Historia General de la Nueva España.* Ed. Robredo, Mexico, 1938.

TORRES, Pedro, *Breve Historia de la Imagen y Primer Culto de Nuestra Señora de la Esperanza....* Morelia, Michoacán, 1949.

VAZQUEZ SANTA ANA, Pbro. Higinio, and Salvador Ortiz VIDALES, *Imagenes Celebres de Mexico.* Mexico, D. F., 1950.

VELASCO, R. P. Fray Felipe, O. F. M., *Novena para celebrar el Mysterio de la Inmaculada Concepción de María Santísima, en la Sagrada Imagen de los Remedios, que se venera en el Convento de N. S. P. S. Francisco de la Villa de S. Juan Tzitáquaro, Provincia y Obispado de Michoacán.* 2a. Ed., Mexico City, 1762.

VETANCUR, Fray Agustín de, O. F. M., *Chrónica de la Provincia del Santo Evangelio de Mexico: 4a Parte del Teatro Mexicano de los succesos Religiosos.* Mexico City, 1697.

VILAPLANA, Fray Hermenegildo, O. F. M., *Historico y Sagrado Novenario de la milagrosa Imagen de Nuestra Señora del Pueblito.* Reimp., El Pueblito, Querétaro, 1954.

VILLANUEVA, L. G., S. J., *La Inmaculada del Tepeyac.* Mexico, D. F., 1931.